Feu d'Amour

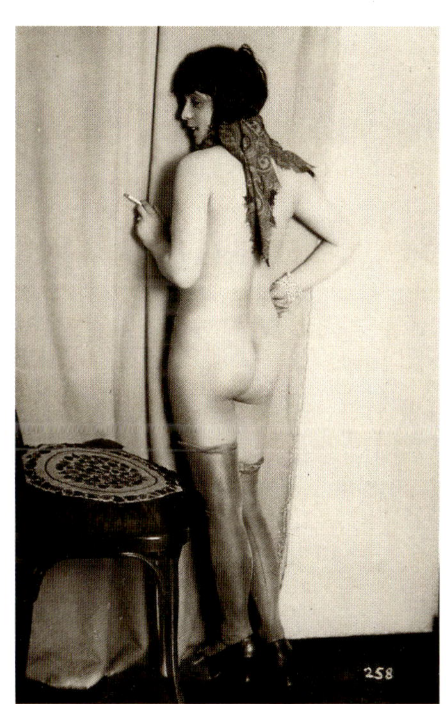

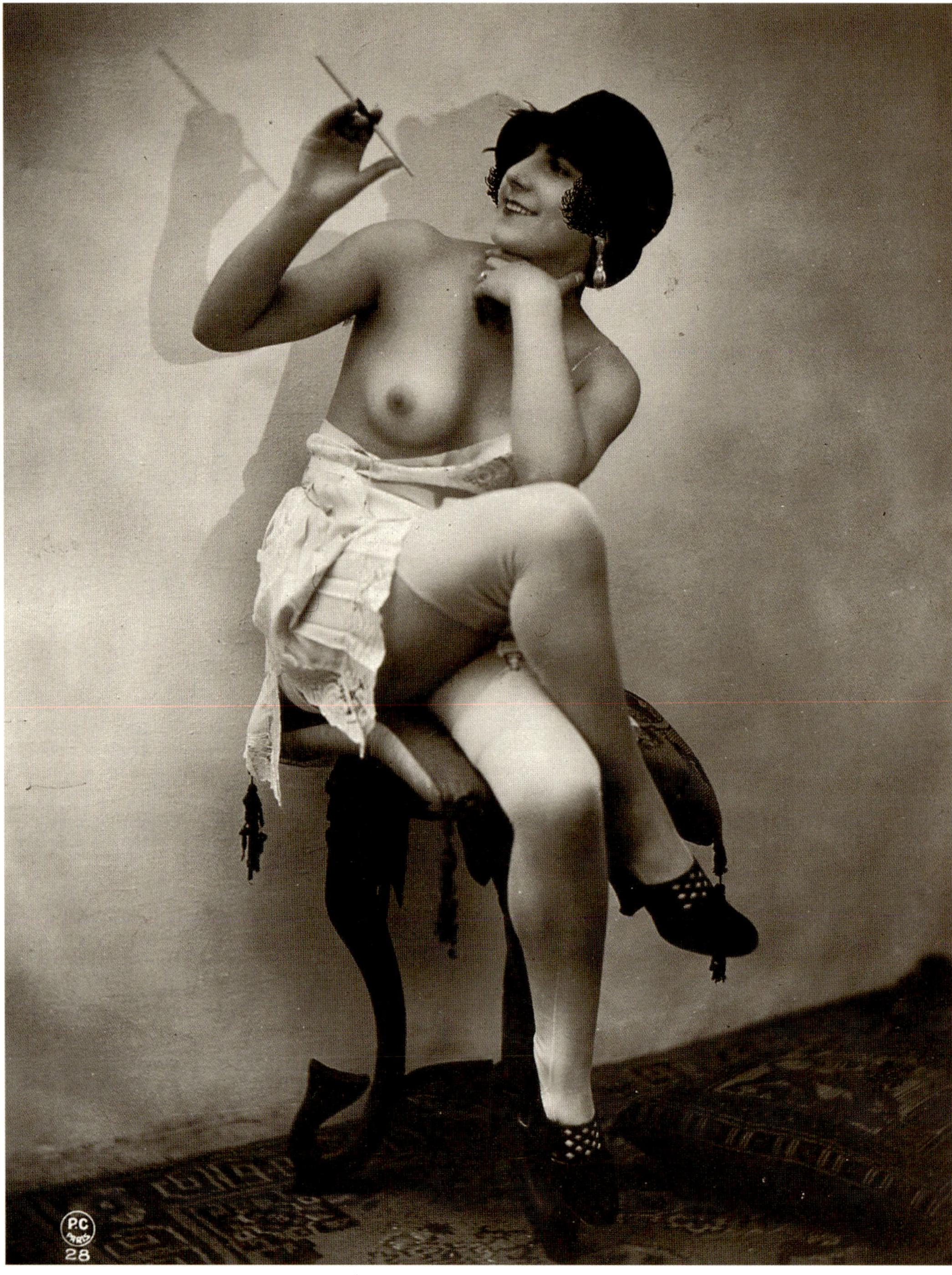
P.C
28

Michael Koetzle / Uwe Scheid

Feu d'Amour

Seductive Smoke

Benedikt Taschen

The photographic material used in this volume
stems from the Uwe Scheid Collection, Überherrn

This book was printed on 100% chlorine-free bleached paper in accordance with the TCF standard.

Hohenzollernring 53, D-50672 Köln

Design: Kühle und Mozer, Cologne
Cover design: Angelika Muthesius, Cologne
Translated and typeset by ITR International Translation Resources Ltd., London

Printed in Portugal
ISBN 3-8228-8661-0
GB

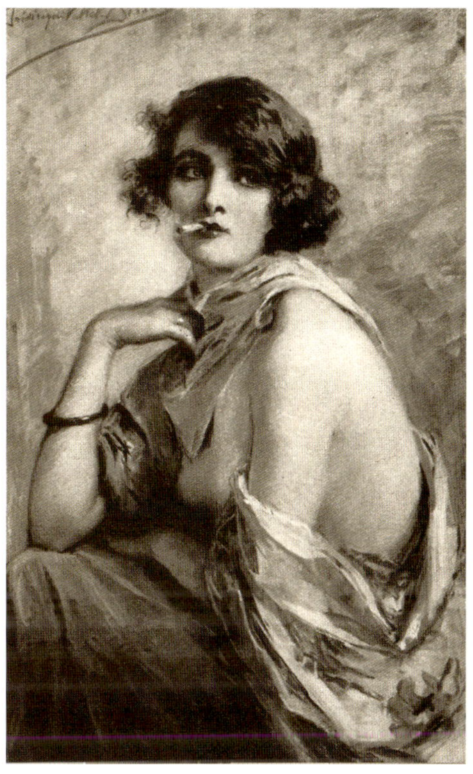

From its earliest beginnings, art has drawn deeply on the erotic impulse. The sacred flame of art was kindled by the fire of love. The goddess of beauty is also the goddess of love. It was the burning desire to depict his longed-for beloved that made man into an artist. This, and only this, spurred him on to recreate the beauty of the female body, which enthralled first his eye and then his senses, and to capture it in pictorial form.

The Erotic in Photography, 1931

Feu d'amour

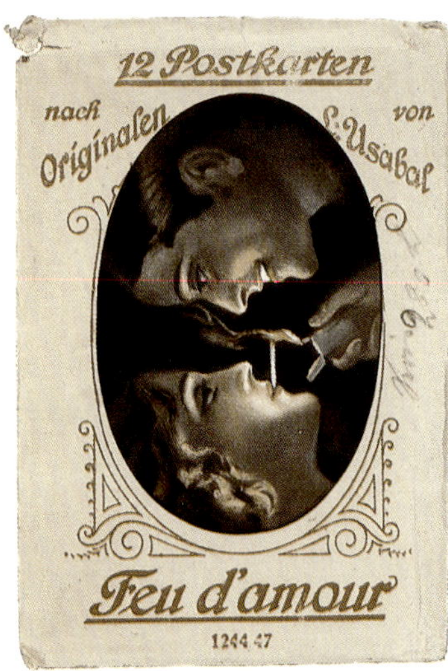

Feu d'amour
Title of a booklet of postcards, c.1920

Observations on smoking and eroticism, tobacco use and emancipation c.1920

Our discovery is scarcely bigger than the palm of the human hand. One of those cheap booklets, still used today to sell picture postcards in sets of six, ten, or twelve. The cover, designed in the style of its time, promises a dozen cards though only four have survived. Framed within an oval vignette we find a visual foretaste of the contents, already hinted at by the French title: *Feu d'amour – Fire of Love.* The story offered is a simple one, conveyed through the medium of graphic illustration still dominant in the consumer advertising of the 1920s. Evening. A couple meet. They move closer, in the pale glow of a lit cigarette. He smokes. She smokes. They look deep into each other's eyes. Of course, the implication is of a "happy ending", a concept as alien to the modern viewer as all the other vanished thematic furniture of six or seven decades ago.

The title *Feu d'amour* acts as leitmotif for a photographic series which owes its existence not to chance, nor to scholarly interest, nor to the good taste of the art connoisseur, but to the erotic interest of the private collector. The earliest photograph, a tinted daguerreotype, probably dates from around 1850. Most of the images come from the '20s and '30s and are primarily postcards. However, there are also 18 x 24 cm silver-gelatine prints, plus reproductions from contemporary magazines such as *Pages folles* or *Sex Appeal.* In chronological terms, Werner Bokelberg's *Pin Up* (1977) or Tina Bara's *Portrait of Ulrike* (1989) mark the end of a genre which, although at first sight merely bizarre, is in fact – from a cultural and historical point of view – highly illuminating.

Apart from Robert Doisneau's "nudge-and-wink" contribution on the subject of male fantasies, Man Ray's extreme close-surveillance study and Richard Avedon's portrait of the ageing Marlene Dietrich together with the works by Bokelberg and Bara already mentioned, all the photographs share one characteristic: their trivial, exploitative purpose. The inspiration for the largely anonymous creators of these images lay not in the general art form of the nude, but in pure eroticism; eroticism of a sometimes voluptuous, sometimes vulgar, sometimes intensely strange kind. The most common medium of publication – the small-format, cheap postcard often produced in massive quantities – in itself indicates the low aesthetic claims of this genre. Today we find their peculiar combination of coy nudity and cigarette smoke puzzling. The anonymous purchaser of the '20s and '30s must have seen them as an ironical, frivolous commentary on the modern woman, smoking and emancipation.

"An entire book could be written under the title: *On the Emancipation of Women through the Cigarette*," noted Delphine de Girardin in 1844 in her *Chroniques Parisiennes.* Since then, the notion of the cigar or cigarette in a woman's hand has become imbued with an extraordinary ambivalence. Already reflected in nineteenth-century works of literature, art and photography, this becomes particularly evident in the work of the New Objectivity painters around 1925. Here, in the work of Otto Dix and George Grosz, Jeanne Mammen and Christian Schad, Karl Hubbuch and Rudolf Schlichter, who again and again chose women with cigarettes as subjects of their drawings and paintings, nicotine becomes a metaphor, a symbol: as expressive of degradation as of emancipation. Grosz had a preference for caricaturing common whores and worn-out old madames with cigarettes in their hands (see his series *Ecce Homo*, 1921, and *Bankruptcy [Die Pleite]*, 1923), but Hubbuch (see *Twice Hilde [Zweimal Hilde]*, 1923) and Schad (see *Sonja*, 1928) depict their subjects as overwhelmingly representative of the type known as the "new woman", shown in the modish combination of Eton crop, knee-length skirt and cigarette.

Perhaps the best-known example of this genre is Dix's portrait of the Berlin journalist Sylvia von Harden. In this picture, painted in 1926 and now in the Musée national d'art moderne in Paris, nothing is left out: the gamin hairstyle (a common theme of contemporary cartoon as in Karl Arnold's contribution to *Simplicissimus*, *Lotte at the Parting of the Ways [Lotte am*

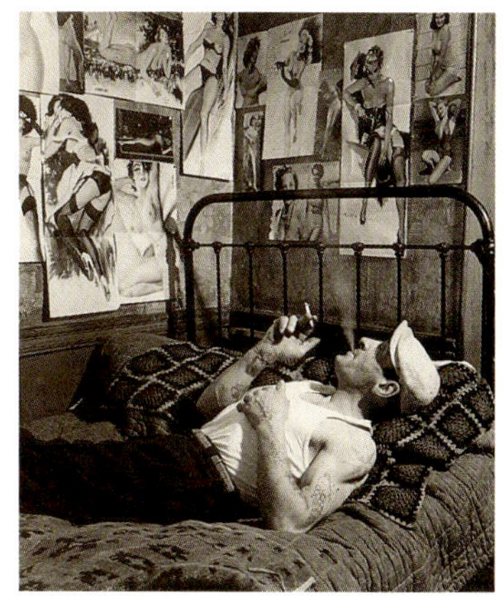

Robert Doisneau
Dream Creatures, 1952

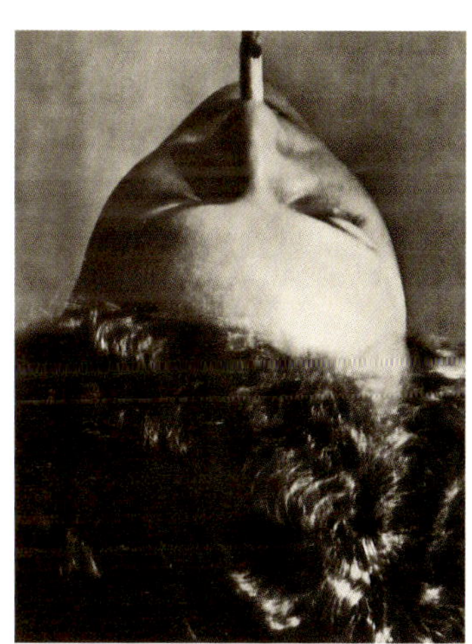

Man Ray
Head, 1923

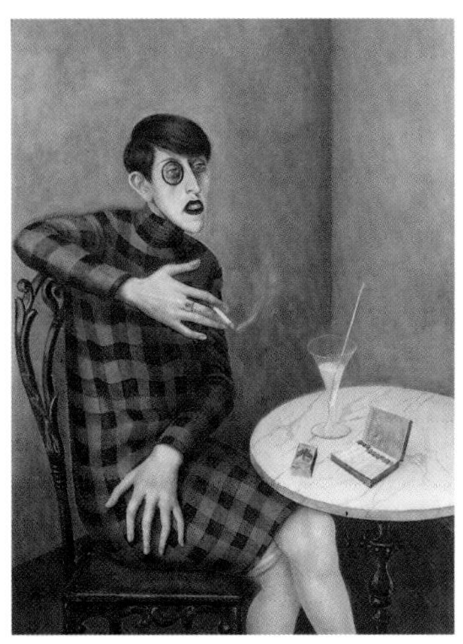

Otto Dix
Sylvia von Harden, 1926

Scheideweg], 1925), the short dress and rolled-down stockings, the cigarette, and even the monocle so favoured by progressive women of the time. And, of course, we must not forget that she is ostentatiously seated at a café table without an escort. Dix discovered her here, in some Berlin dive of the mid-1920s. He just had to paint her, he announced to the astonished woman, and replied when she asked him why, "You stand for an entire era."

The link between smoking and emancipation can be traced back to the early nineteenth century. Possibly the first photographic evidence, and in any case an important document, is supplied by Lola Montez. It was well-known that Montez was not her name nor was she of Spanish descent. We see her having a portrait taken at the Boston studio of Southworth & Hawes, probably in 1851. Her liaison with the King of Bavaria ended three years ago. Ludwig has abdicated, the dancer has left Munich. Since 1851 she has been living in the USA. Montez: a self-confident *femme fatale* on a quest for happiness, personal autonomy, an independent life beyond the well-trodden paths of bourgeois existence.

The daguerreotype in question (16.5 x 21.6 cm) shows a well-groomed woman of 30. The simple furnishings of the studio are in complete accord with the austere aesthetic standards of early portrait photography. Montez, seen here in a three-quarter-length portrait, leans against a draped pedestal, not least to prevent blurring during the lengthy exposure-time required. In her dress, hairstyle and self-contained demeanour she could pass for a lady, if it weren't for the cigarette, which stands out particularly effectively against the black of her gloved hand. The fact that it is unlit underlines its function as a prop, deliberately introduced as a symbol of provocation. The cigarette, for all its insignificant size, is actually the determining factor in the composition, the focal point to which the viewer's gaze is involuntarily drawn – the *punctum*, as Roland Barthes would describe it in the language of semiotics.

George Sand, the French writer and *enfant terrible* of the salons in the 1850s, is reported to have smoked in public. What is more, she wore men's clothes, right down to the cravat, hat and boots. Just how much of a stir the subject of women and smoking caused during the 1840s and 1850s can be seen in numerous cartoons. Prominent artists such as Grandville still show their women with pipes and cigars (see his cartoon *The Emancipation of Women*). The women may be smoking but they are still seen in a male-dominated environment and still wear corsets and crinolines. Far-sighted observers, however, have already glimpsed in "tobacco mania" presentiments of a much broader, more significant development. "The emancipation of women is progressing in a curious way in Germany, and especially in Berlin, Germany's most intellectual city," commented an anonymous critic in the period before the 1848 revolutions. "It is having the most surprising consequences. In the city's most glittering circles, girls of 19 and 20 discuss Guizot, Thiers, the laws of privacy and search, with an assurance that borders on the astounding. Many of these miniature George Sands have already learned not to spurn a cigarette; recently an elegant lady was even seen to stop a cigarette-smoking gentleman on a public street in order to obtain a light for her own. What extraordinary prospects lie before us! How long will it be before they start wearing trousers, whipping their menfolk into the kitchen and nursing their babies on horseback! Our emancipated women would take these in their stride! A public coffee house for ladies is about to be opened, and soon they'll be sounding off about the condition of women, while they smoke their little cigars and read the latest newspapers. In short – they'll live like men! How glad Berlin's husbands will be to clutch their darling wives – burning cigarettes and all – to their ardent breasts."

With the technical, industrial and social changes at the end of the 19th century, the role of women in society is transformed. The boundaries of the forbidden and the permissible are pushed back, opening up hitherto unknown prospects of freedom. Not the least important external evidence of this change comes in the world of fashion. Couturiers such as the legendary Paul Poiret are credited with the abolition of the crinoline and the corset and the introduction of a more comfortable, contemporary fashion. This is true only on the most superficial level. In fact, the new style of clothing is dictated by the needs of a society based on manufacturing and service industries. Where women are in demand as

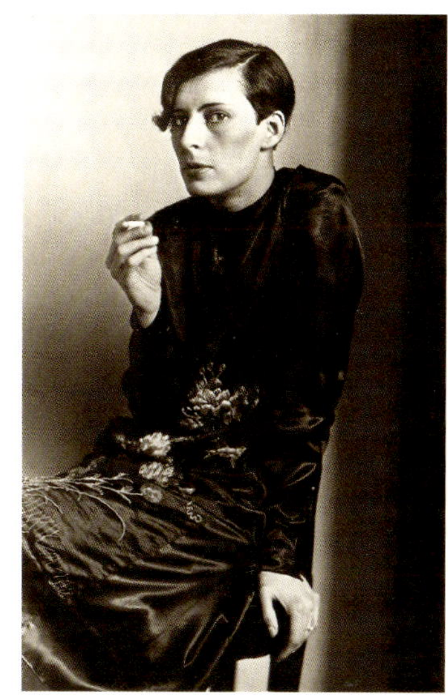

August Sander
Radio Secretary, 1931

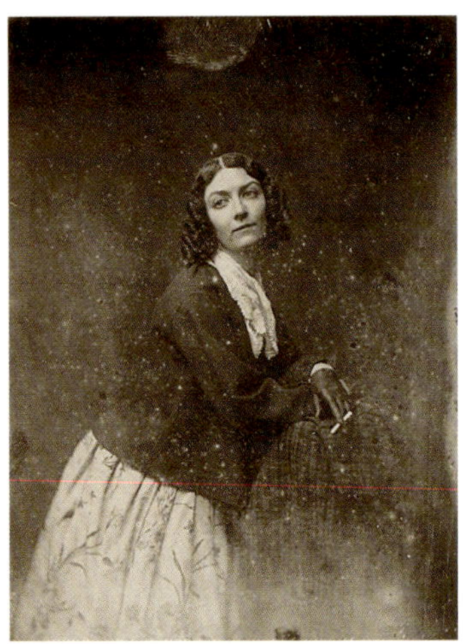

Southworth & Hawes
Lola Montez, 1851

labour in commerce or industry, freedom of movement – in the literal sense – is required, and dress reminiscent of courtly costume becomes obsolete.

In this respect, as in others, the First World War is a major watershed. Women now replace men in the labour market to a dramatic extent, contributing significantly to equality in lifestyle and dress. In 1891 Paul Nadar photographed the transvestite performer and actress Mme Lantelme – in male dress, smoking and with short hair. The social utopia depicted in the role-portraits of the belle epoque has become reality in the world of the big city after 1918. Women wear trousers, play sport, cut their hair. And women smoke – even in the face of disapproval from self-appointed moral guardians such as Emanuele L. M. Meyer, well-known in the early part of the century for a variety of textbooks on sexual issues such as *From Girl to Woman (Vom Mädchen zur Frau)*. "Anyone who is forced to look at these women, with their Eton crops or similar eccentric hairstyles, their short skirts, crossed legs, carelessly blowing smoke-rings and reading the newspaper, cannot but feel sickened," wrote the author in 1924. "And, disheartened, he will say that as long as this type of female is in the ascendant, a new world, with women as a strong exemplary force within it, remains unthinkable."

The phenotype described by Emanuele Meyer has passed into the cultural history of the 20th Century as the "new woman". Walter Serner described her in his novel *The Tigress (Die Tigerin*, 1925). Otto Dix portrayed her in the shape of his Sylvia von Harden. August Sander, whose radio secretary of 1931 is a kind of provincial equivalent of Dix's journalist, has captured her image in photographic form.

In the mid-1920s and early 1930s, the cinema and the illustrated popular press are chiefly responsible for promoting this idea. Rudolf Mosse's press catalogue of 1931 lists no fewer than 47 daily newspapers, 33 suburban dailies, and 50 weekly newspapers for Berlin alone. To this must be added nine illustrated newspapers, five illustrated weekend supplements and dozens of magazines and illustrated monthlies. Among these is the magazine *Die Dame. Deutsches Journal für den verwöhnten Geschmack (The Lady. German Journal for the Discerning)*. Its July 1929 edition was designed by the Polish-French Art Deco artist Tamara de Lempicka, who had herself achieved cult status. In its subject-matter and bold use of perspective, her self-portrait as confident "gentleman driver" to some extent anticipates Robert Doisneau's 1934 advertising photograph for Renault. It is representative of the numerous contemporary photo-reports about "new women", driving, on horseback, active at work and leisure, successful, businesslike, both sporty and cigarette smoking – a combination at that time in no way seen as contradictory, as can be seen markedly in an early fashion photograph by Ernst Sandau (for Gerson, 1921).

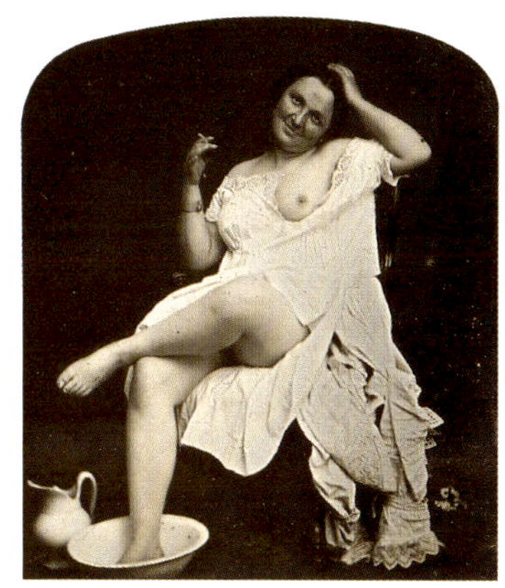

Anonymous
Untitled
Daguerreotype, c.1850

Strictly speaking, the "new woman" was more of a media reality than an accepted part of daily life during the Weimar Republic. Nevertheless, as a phenomenon she does serve to draw attention to a whole wave of emancipatory change, culminating in such achievements as universal female suffrage and the admission of women to universities. The playing of sport by women and their right to smoke in public also emerge from the realm of taboo. During the course of the "social spread of smoking" (Schivelbusch), the cigarette has acquired more of the status of a fashionable accessory. But can the presentation of smoking adapt accordingly? There is still clearly only a thin line between "fashionable/elegant" and "lascivious", not least in the numerous glamour portraits of the '30s and '40s which make conscious play on this ambivalence. In a famous photograph by Alfred Eisenstaedt (1929), Marlene Dietrich, self-confident and decidedly "butch", prominently displays her cigarette, which seems a natural part of "formal dress", like the tail-coat, white tie and top hat. The presentation is no less elegant, but more feminine-worldly, in a photograph by Ray Jones (1940). A Dietrich portrait of 1941 clearly plays up the vamp, emphasises the element and, alongside the slit skirt and bedroom eyes, the cigarette is still an important part of the "equipment", even today. "It belongs with champagne, gambling and love, recklessness, sin, and the poetry of pleasure," wrote the Viennese fin-de-siècle literary figure Paul von Schönthan in this vein. "Its aromatic, fragrant haze, diffusing in delicate rings and clouds, is the perfume of the boudoir."

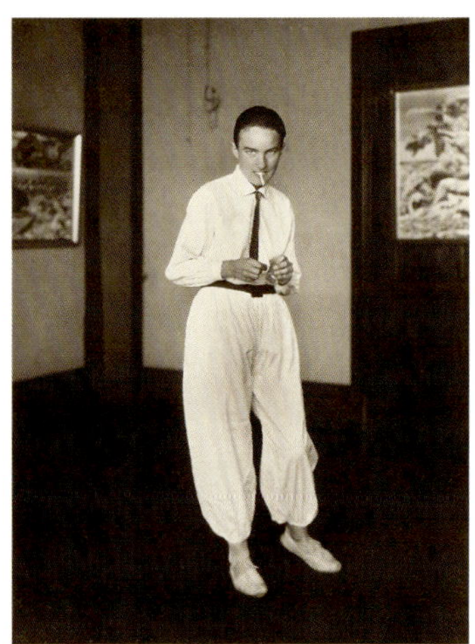

August Sander
Wife of a Painter, 1927

The photographic series introduced here also explores this area of tension between the sophisticated and the obscene and between emancipation and provocation. The anonymous stereo-card, probably from before 1900, of two "loose" girls roguishly smoking, and the picture postcard of an unnamed lady define the extremes. The profile of the lady is very much in the tradition of studio photography. Dressed in twentieth-century clothes, she typifies the new, self-confident, sporty, emancipated woman, for whom the elegantly-displayed cigarette complete with tip has become an indispensable accessory, a prop for the public persona (cf. p. 39). The theme of the stereo-card (cf. p. 23), on the other hand, in a sense turns the equation of smoking and emancipation on its head. Here the cigarette is no longer a symbol of the confident "new woman" but evidence of "ruin", of love for sale. The progressive image gives way to an older cliché: woman as whore and as an object in a double sense – seen first by the camera's lens, and later by the gaze of a male observer, in whose stereoscopic vision the little boudoir scene will be reassembled in three-dimensional form.

We do not know who took the photograph. Most of the photographs reproduced here were anonymous, with good reason. Until well into the middle of our century, the production and distribution of nude photographs – if they served no scientific or artistic purpose – was illegal. Even in a comparatively liberal country such as France, which was in fact the centre of erotic photography, prosecutions were repeatedly brought against dealers and photographers. What was probably the first of these took place in Paris in July 1851. In court were the photographer Felix Jacques-Antoine Moulin (c.1810 – c.1870) and his dealer, Malacrida. "Mr Malacrida," the judgement declared, "optician, on whose property a great quantity of pictures was seized – images so obscene that even to publish the titles that appear in the charge-sheet would render one subject to prosecution for the distribution of indecent material – is sentenced to one year in prison and 500 francs fine. The widow René, supplier of the daguerreotypes, is sentenced to two months' imprisonment and a 200-franc fine. Mr Jacques-Antoine Moulin, author of the daguerreotypes, is sentenced to a month in prison and is fined 100 francs."

Of course, the erotic image was not something that suddenly sprang into existence with the invention of photography. Nevertheless, in August 1839, the introduction and publication of the technical process for fixing such images gave the realm of the "obscene" a quite new dimension. It was not so much the quantity of nude material and its capacity for mass-distribution. Far more significant was the actual quality of the new process, the phenomenology of a technique by which an erotic subject no longer represented the figment of an artist's imagination but the result of an actual event. For the nineteenth-century public, to view an erotic daguerreotype was to participate in the nakedness of a complete stranger. Monstrous, but at the same time profoundly fascinating. The most intimate thing became public, nudity became a commodity.

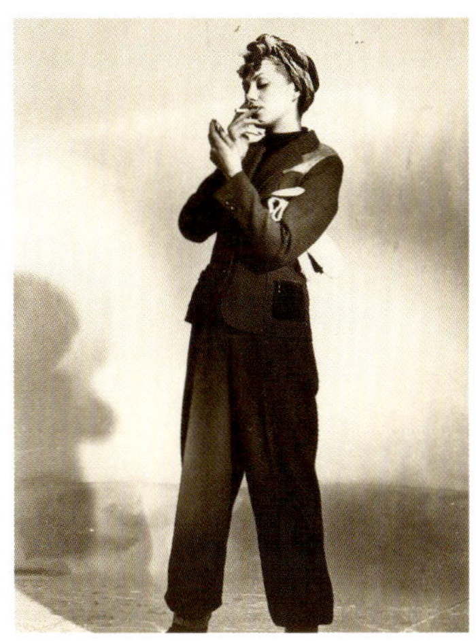

Anonymous
Green Trouser Suit, 1941

What had been accessible to only a few in the age of the daguerreotype – daguerreotypes were one-off artifacts and correspondingly expensive – was transformed into a true mass-phenomenon by the improvements in the negative-positive process that occurred around the middle of the nineteenth century. As cheap showcases for the art of the erotic, stereo-cards and visiting cards became especially popular after 1850. From 1870 onwards the picture-postcard was also available. Its ready-made, pocket-sized format has made it a popular purveyor of clandestine erotic fantasies right up to the present day.

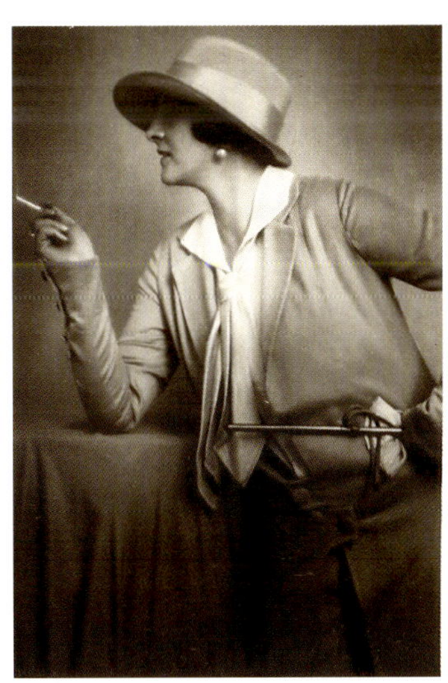

Setzer
Untitled, c.1920/30

The mass-produced erotic material was accompanied by a chorus of warning voices, by laws and regulations intended to stem the flood of "trash and filth". In the final analysis these achieved nothing, except to show that the terrain of the "obscene" in no way conformed to strict cartographical laws. What was yesterday stigmatized as pornography today adorns the covers of the magazines at our local newsstand. Something which is taboo in one culture is hardly even considered erotic in another. That which arouses one person leaves another cold. The erotic remains a variable quantity, dependent on historic, cultural, social and psychological factors.

If we grace the sequences of pictures shown here with the epithet "erotic", then it is with an eye to their iconography, to a specific type of portrayal which remains as distinct from the nude as

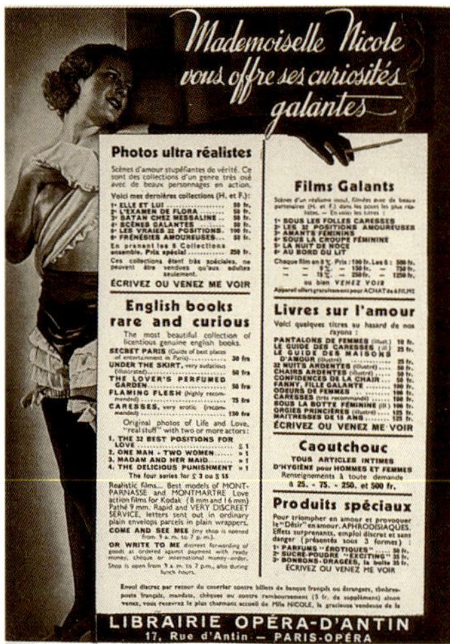

Advertising poster
1920s

an art form as from blatant obscenity. If the "artistic" nude strives for an ideal of ultimate nakedness, the risqué genre resorts to all the old games of revelation and concealment, promise and fulfilment in its attempt to rouse the viewer's imagination. Where the nude photograph engages in a kind of "interior monologue", the erotic portrayal seeks dialogue with the camera, or with the anonymous consumer. The erotic photograph therefore has the enticing gaze into the lens, the come-hither gesture, the sweet smile, the illusion of intimate togetherness. What the erotic photograph merely promises, the "pornographic" fulfils so forcefully that many viewers are repelled rather than aroused. Whereas the pleasure in the artistic nude arises for the most part from its self-imposed restraint, in the erotic photograph no accessory is too outré so long as it serves the projected aim of sexual arousal. Stockings, straps, high-heeled shoes, shawls, veils, jewellery, feathers, fans, and underwear have thus been among the basic accoutrements of erotic photography since its earliest days. Since 1840 curtains and drapes, carpets and small items of furniture have served to re-create the atmosphere of the boudoir. Mirrors are used to multiply the erotic image or capture outrageous revelations. Couches and chairs are used to support bizarre poses. Around 1900, the cigarette was added as an element with clear symbolic content. "Until well into the 1930s the cigarette tip or exceptionally long cigarette-holder turned the female act of smoking into an almost theatrical form of self-dramatisation," observes Schivelbusch in his *History of Stimulants (Geschichte der Genußmittel)*. "From a cultural, historical and psycho-analytical point of view it would be tempting to regard the oral-erotic element in this self-dramatisation as a specific expression of the period between 1890 and 1930."

Even today the cigarette has lost neither its many-faceted function nor its symbolic quality in the field of erotic fantasies and pictorial presentation. For recent proof we need look only to the international fashion photographer, Peter Lindbergh. In Paris at the end of 1992 he exhibited 40 *Smoking Women*: portraits, nudes, fashion shots of highly-paid models, from Tatiana Patitz to Lynne Koester, from Linda Evangelista to Helena Christensen. What united them, apart from the cigarettes in their hands or mouths, was youthful, flawless beauty. For this, too, is an essential element of the erotic photograph. While artists of the nude in the twentieth century have certainly highlighted the worn-out, vulnerable, damaged human body, the erotic photograph has stayed faithful to its supreme commandment: depiction of the current bodily ideal. But to quote Walter Serner from his *Pocket Guide for Swindlers (Handbrevier für Hochstapler,* 1927): "When you really get down to it, the only thing that counts in love is young, fresh flesh."

Michael Koetzle

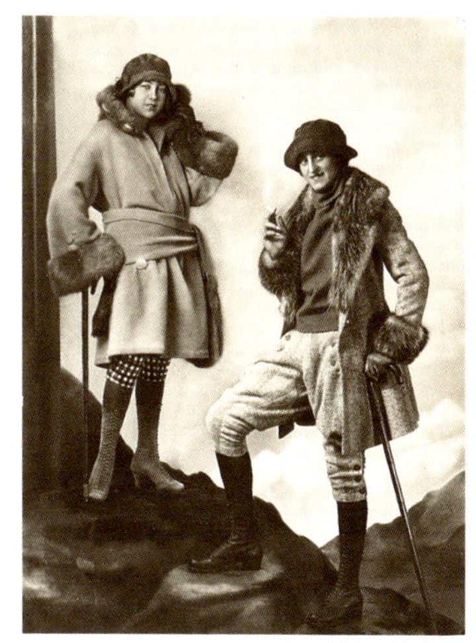

Ernst Sandau
Sportswear for Hiking, 1921

To calm my contented sighs
nothing is better than the abyss of your bed.

Charles Baudelaire

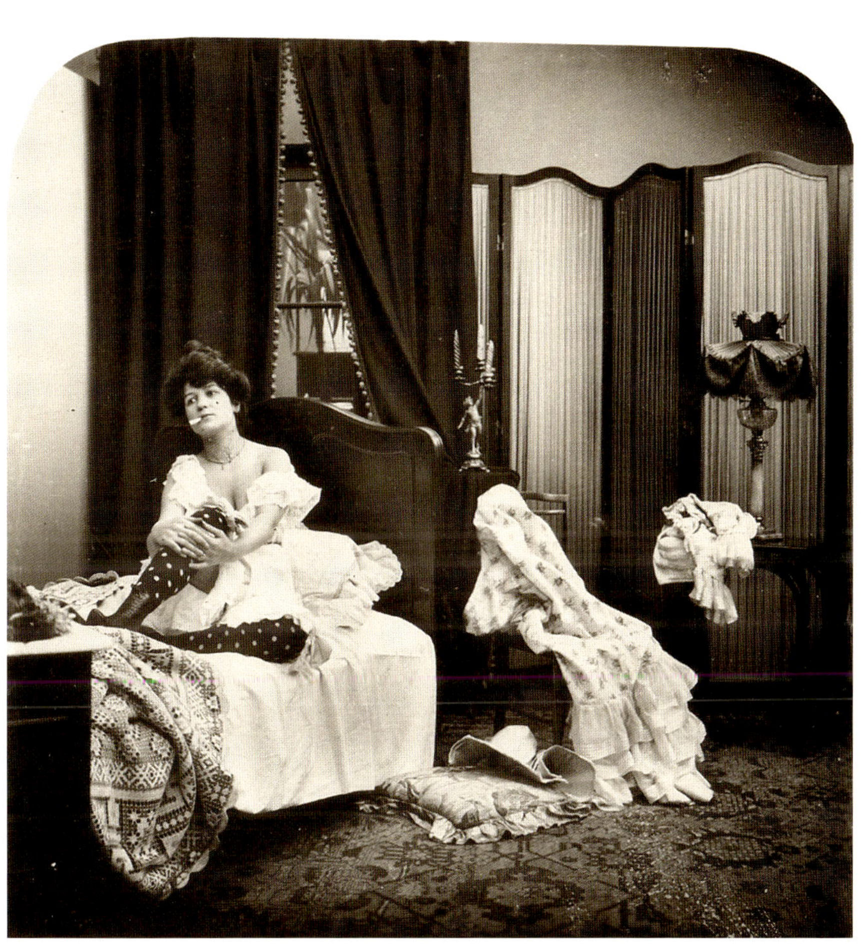

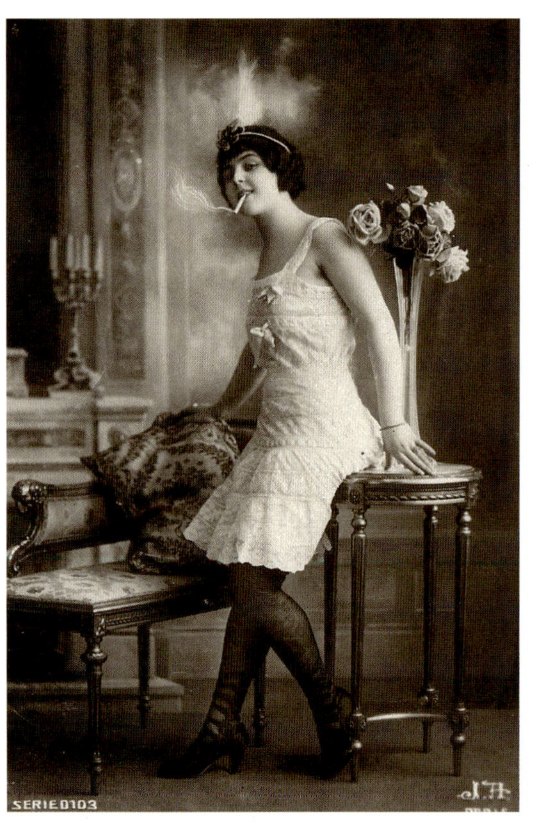
SERIE D103

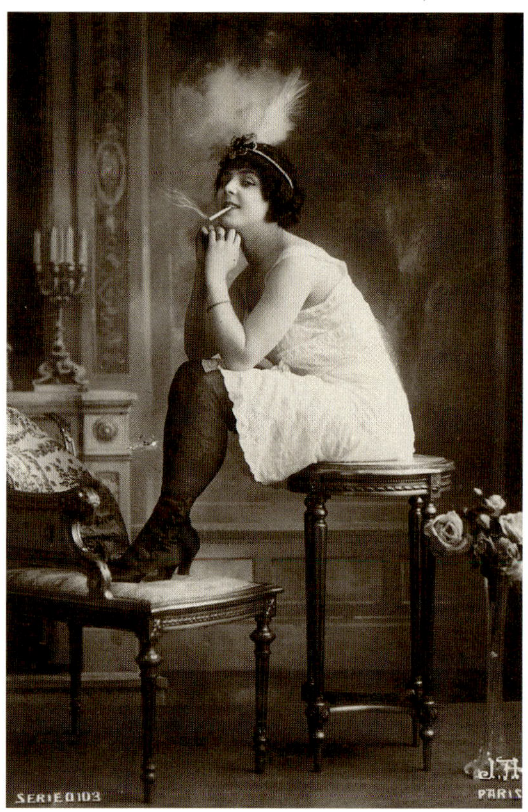
SERIE D103
PARIS

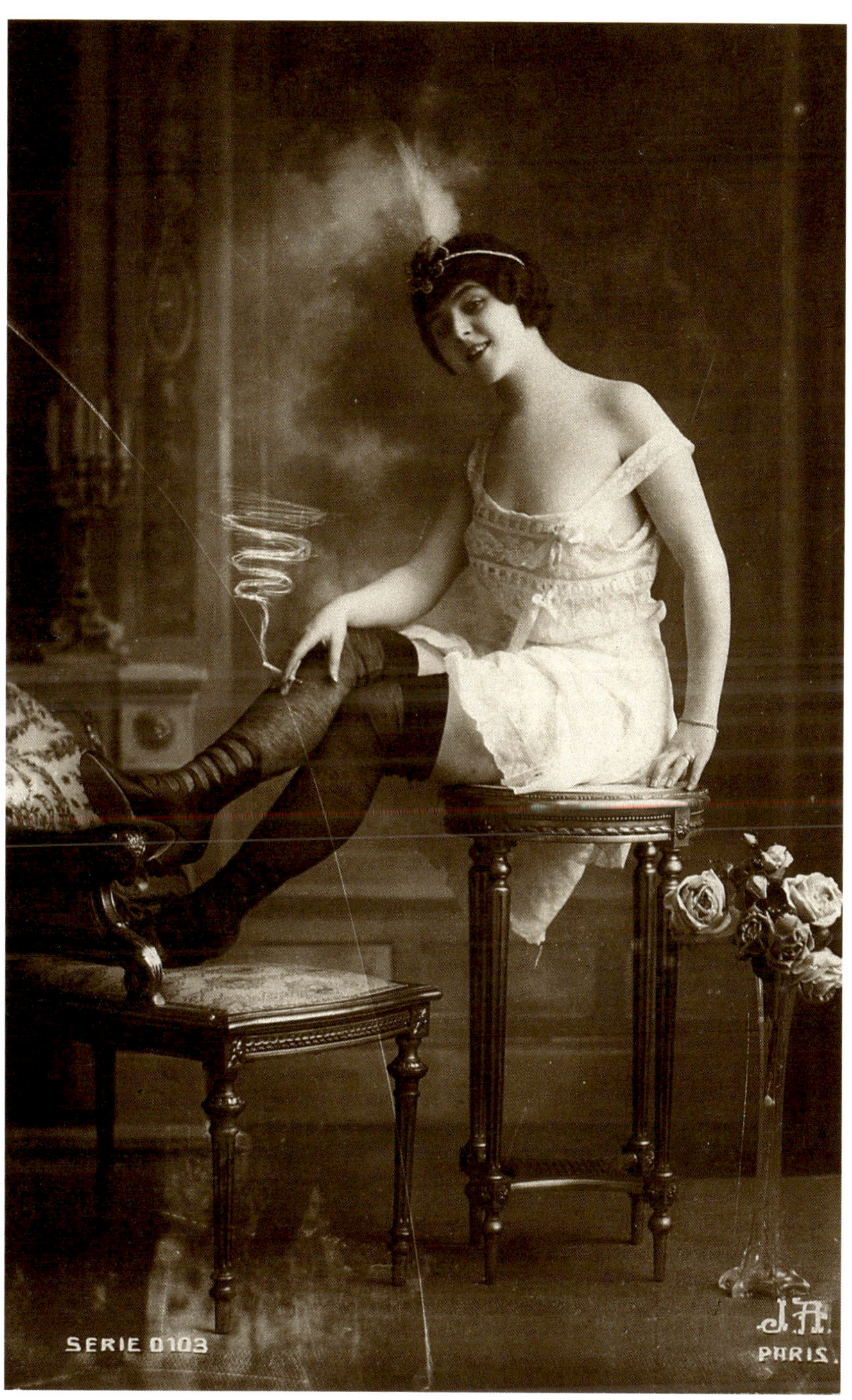
SERIE 0103
J.A.
PARIS.

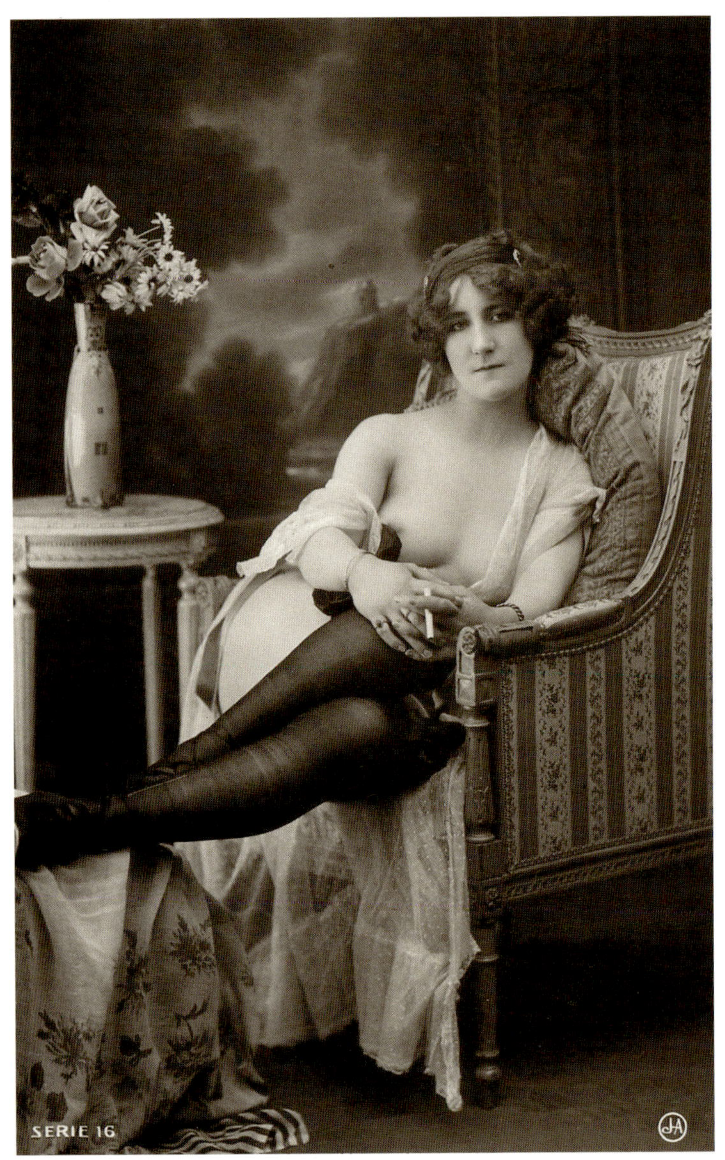
SERIE 16
JA

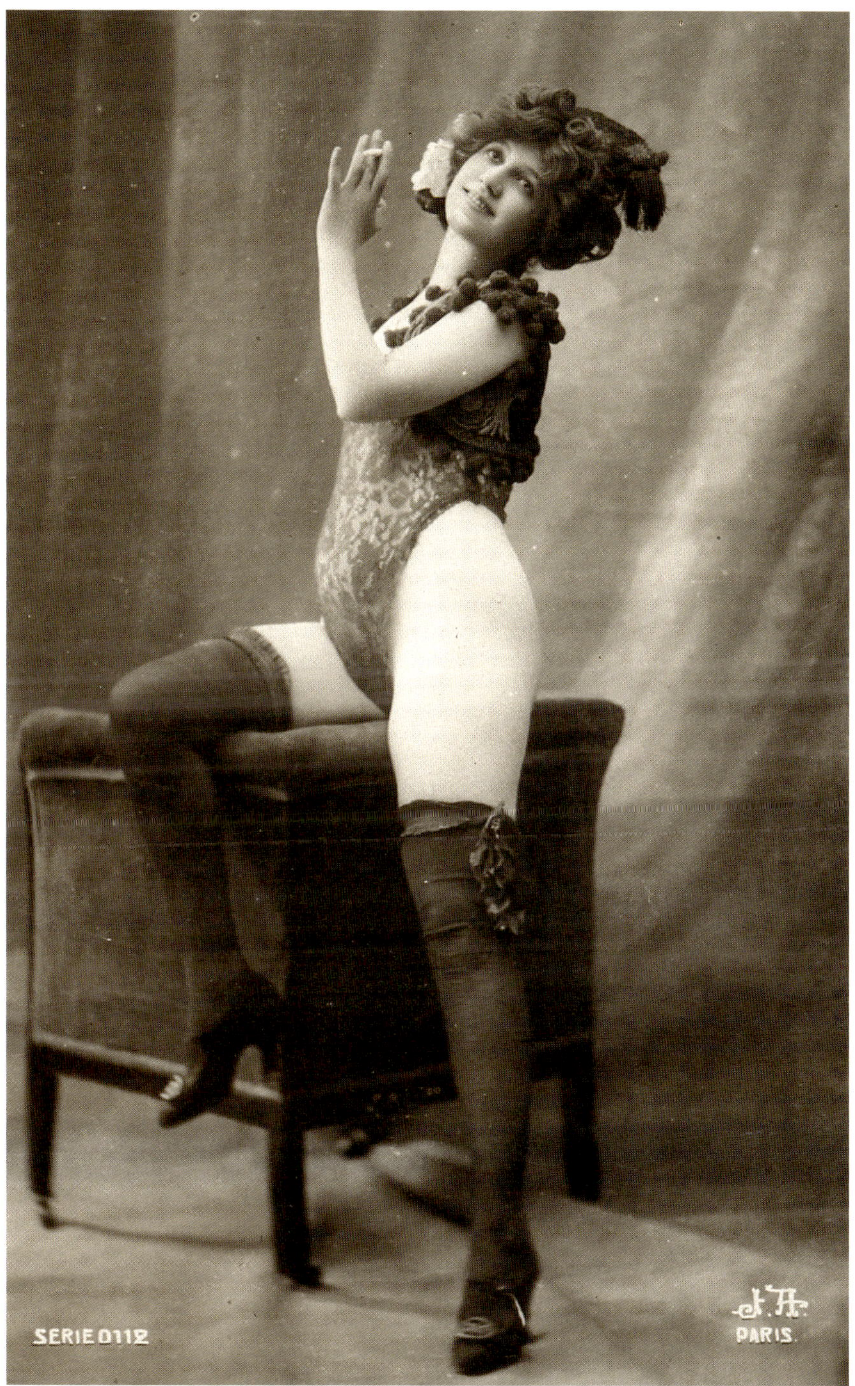
SERIE 0112
J.A.
PARIS.

You alone please me; not carelessly,
but out of inclination I loved your youth
and, therefore, I like my passion.

Pierre de Ronsard

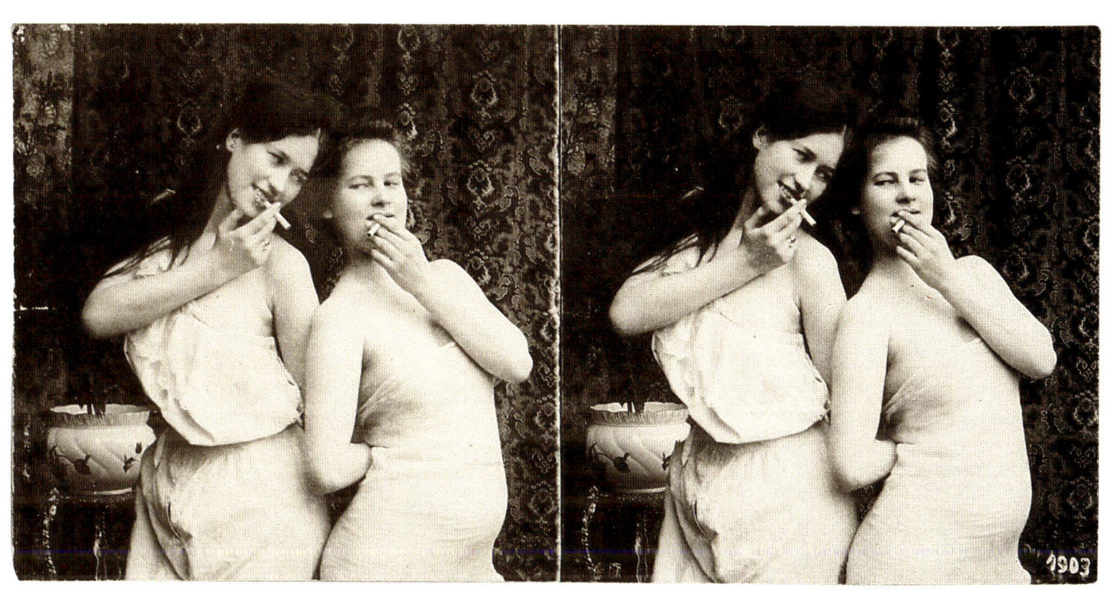
1903

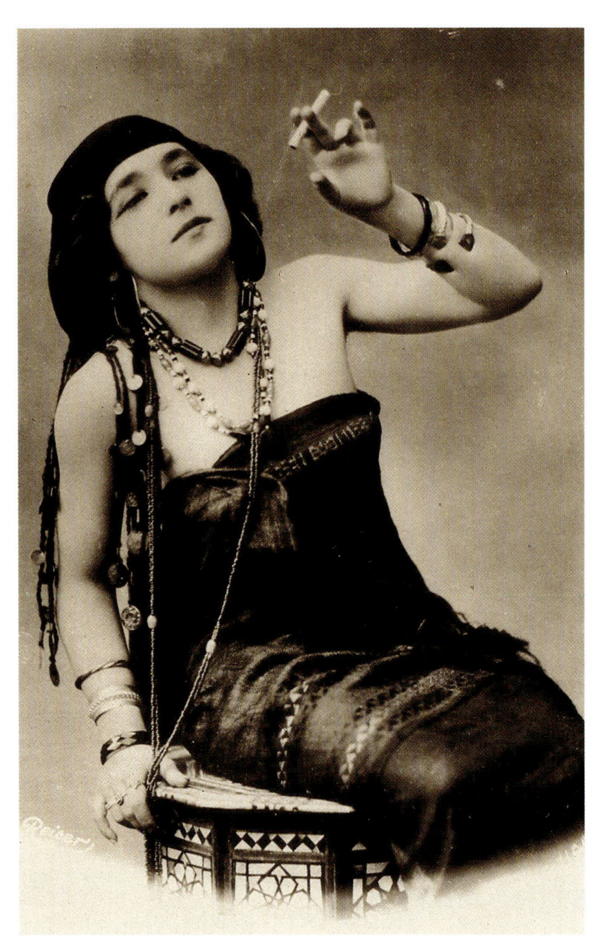
Reiser

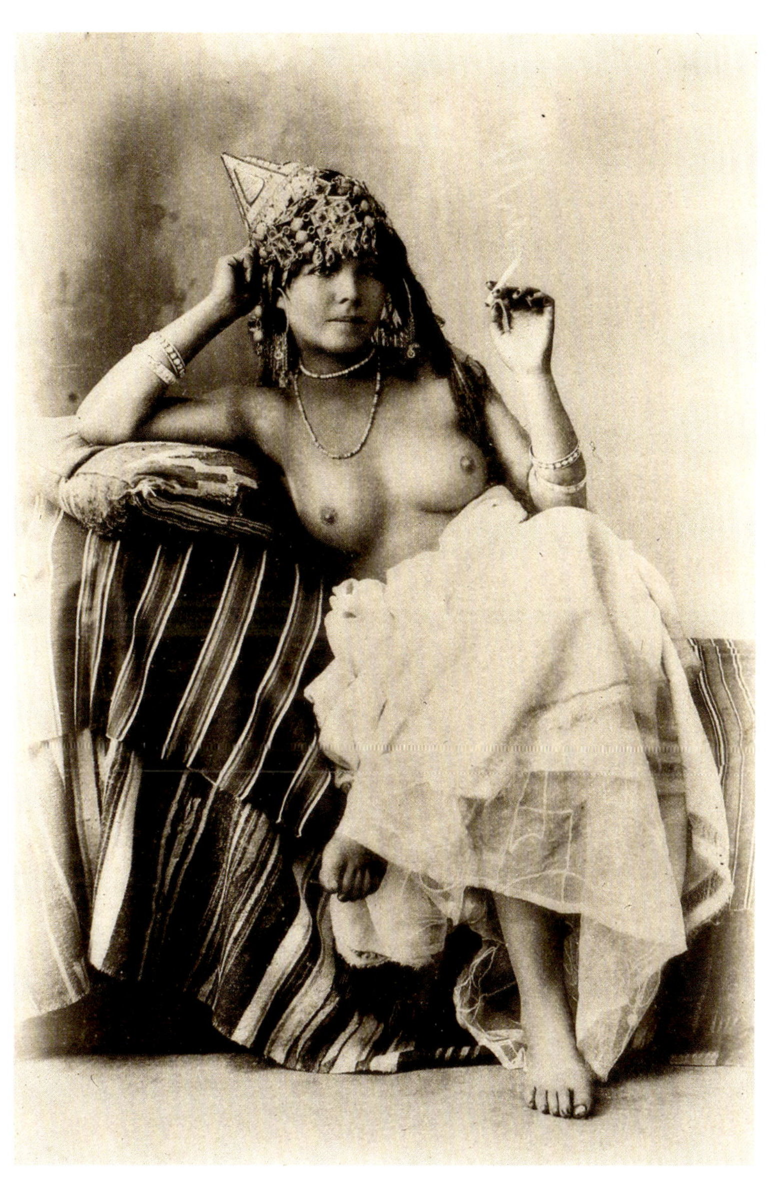

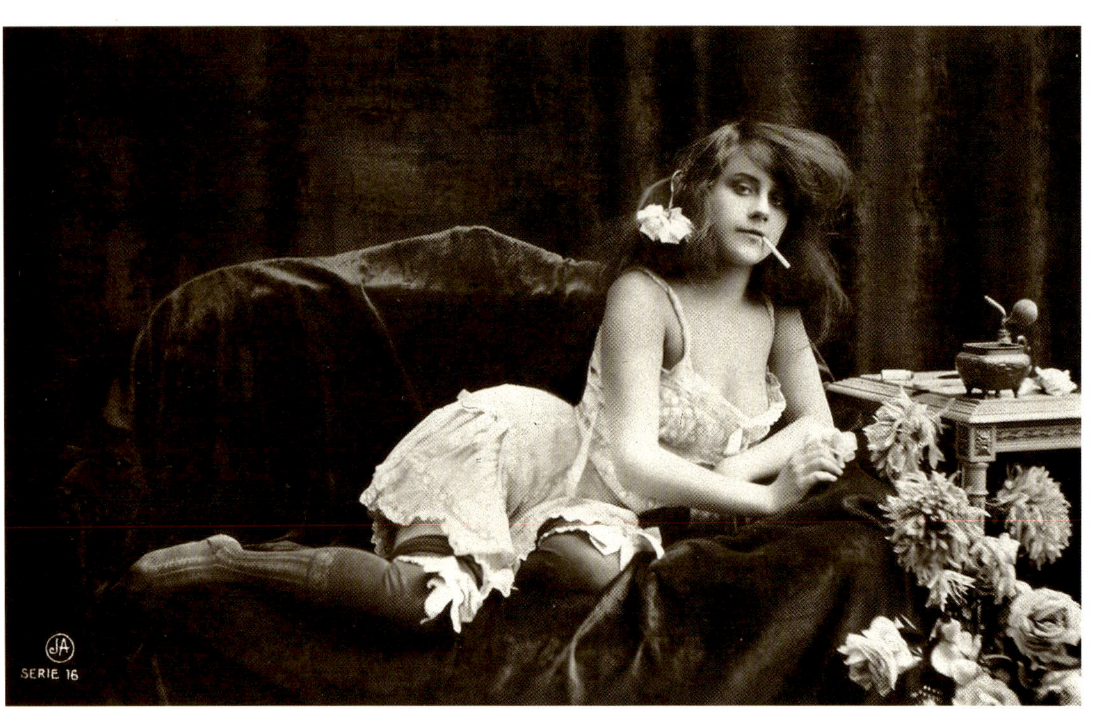
JA
SERIE 16

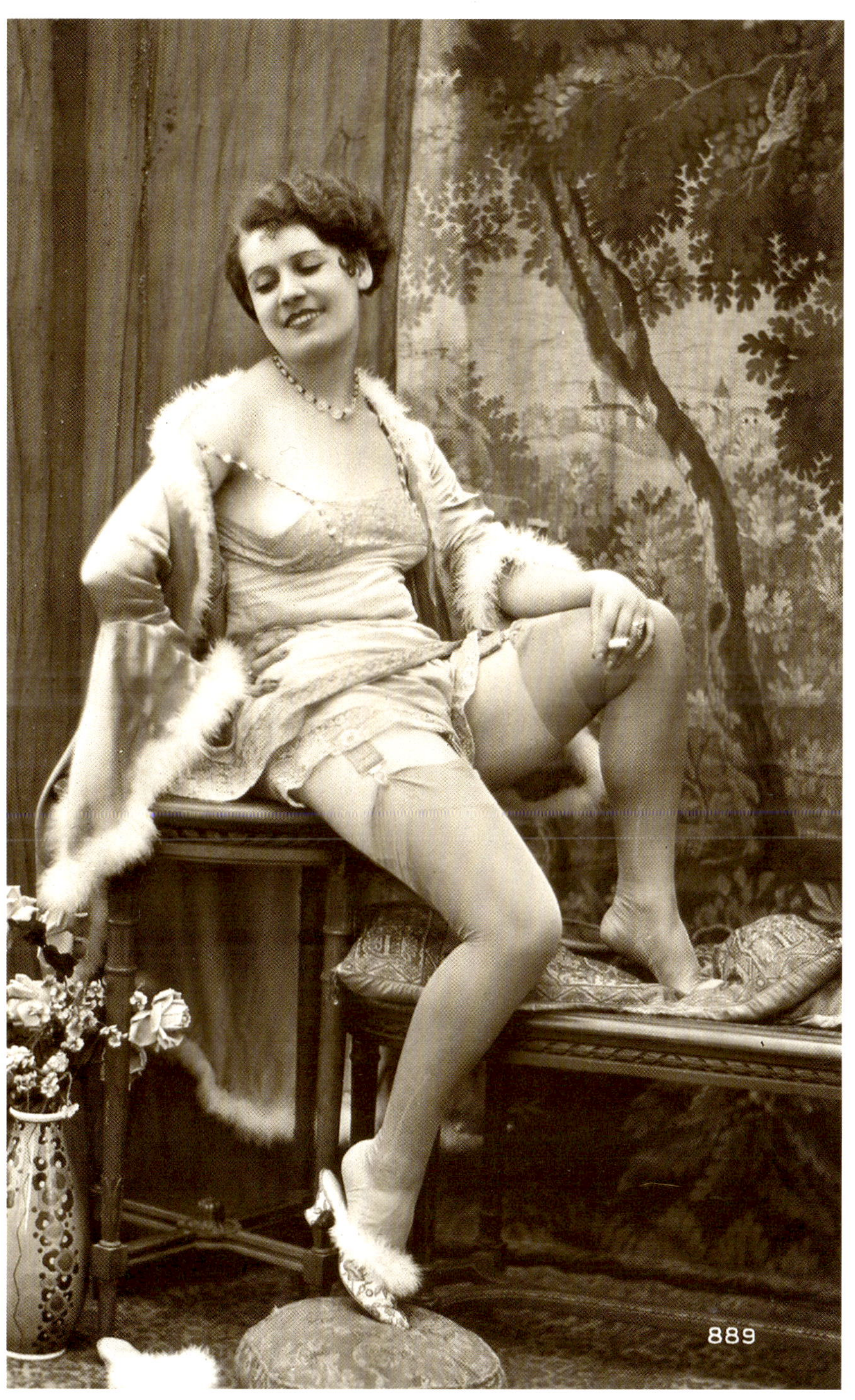
889

Nothing is better than to live according to one's taste.

François Villon

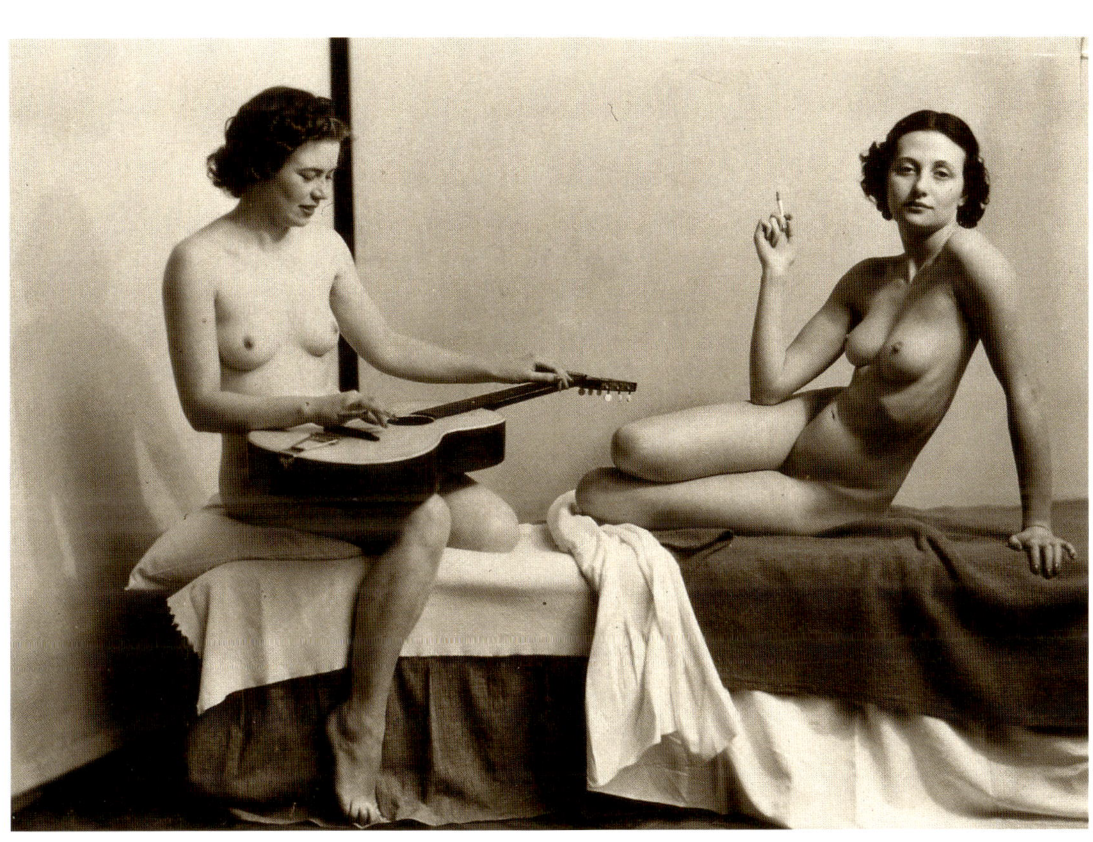

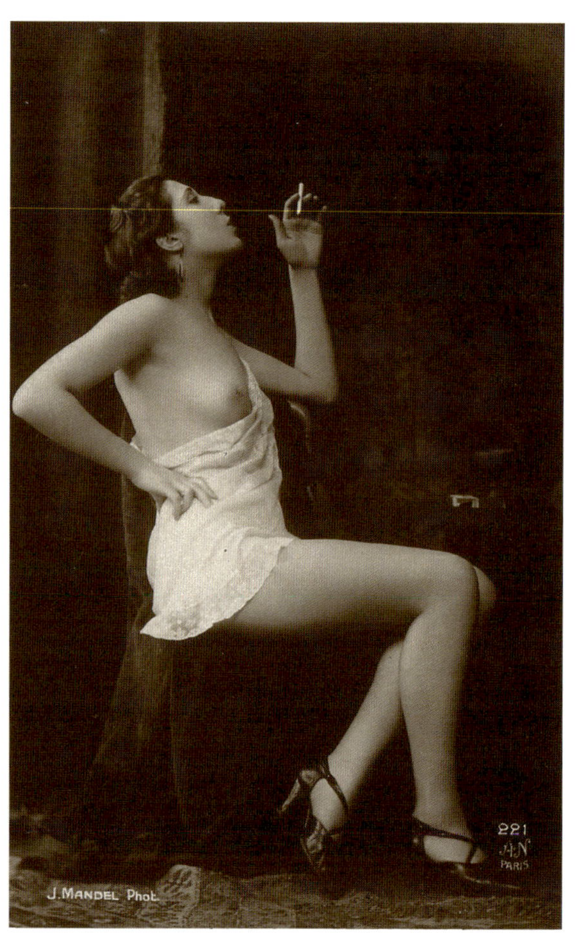
J. MANDEL Phot.
221
PARIS

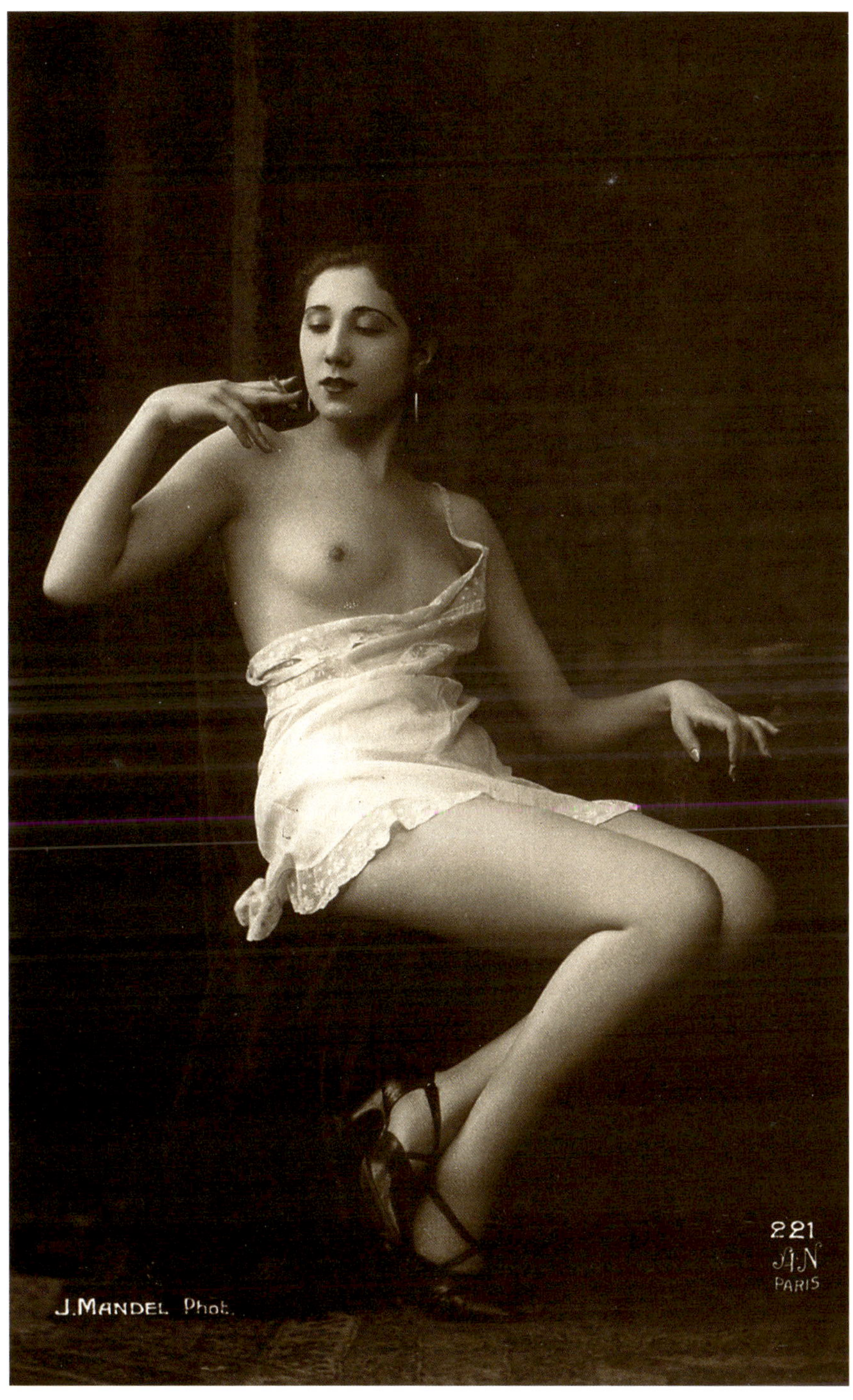
221
PARIS
J.MANDEL Phot.

To extinguish the flames of their love,
flames, fiercer than those of the blessed Anthony.

François Villon

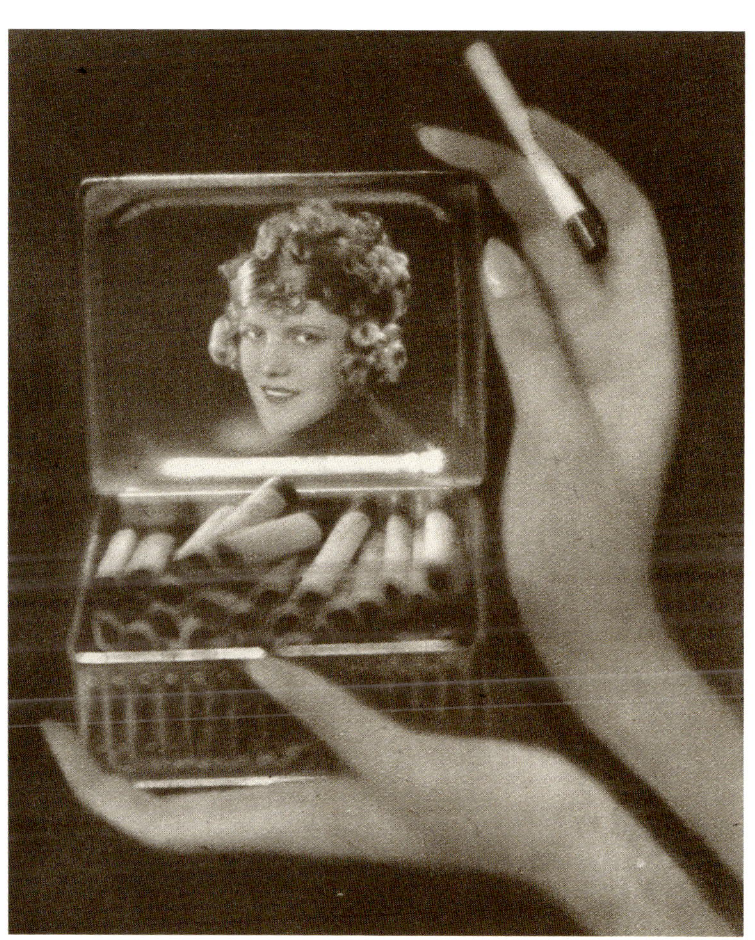

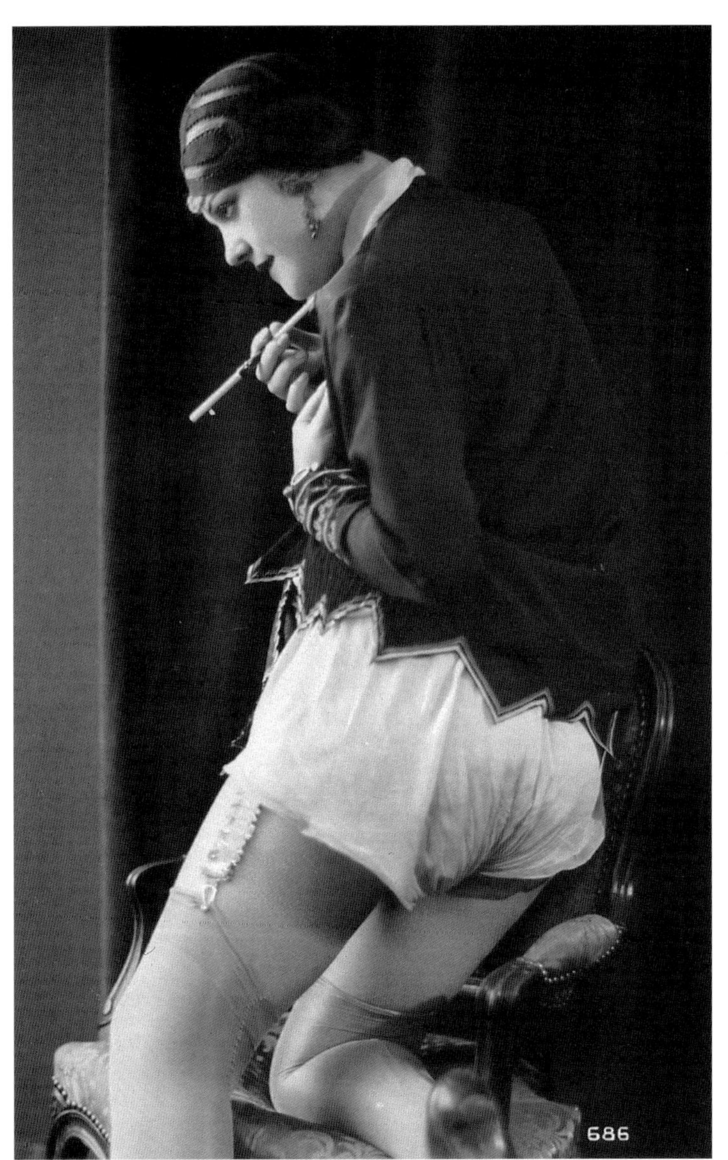
686

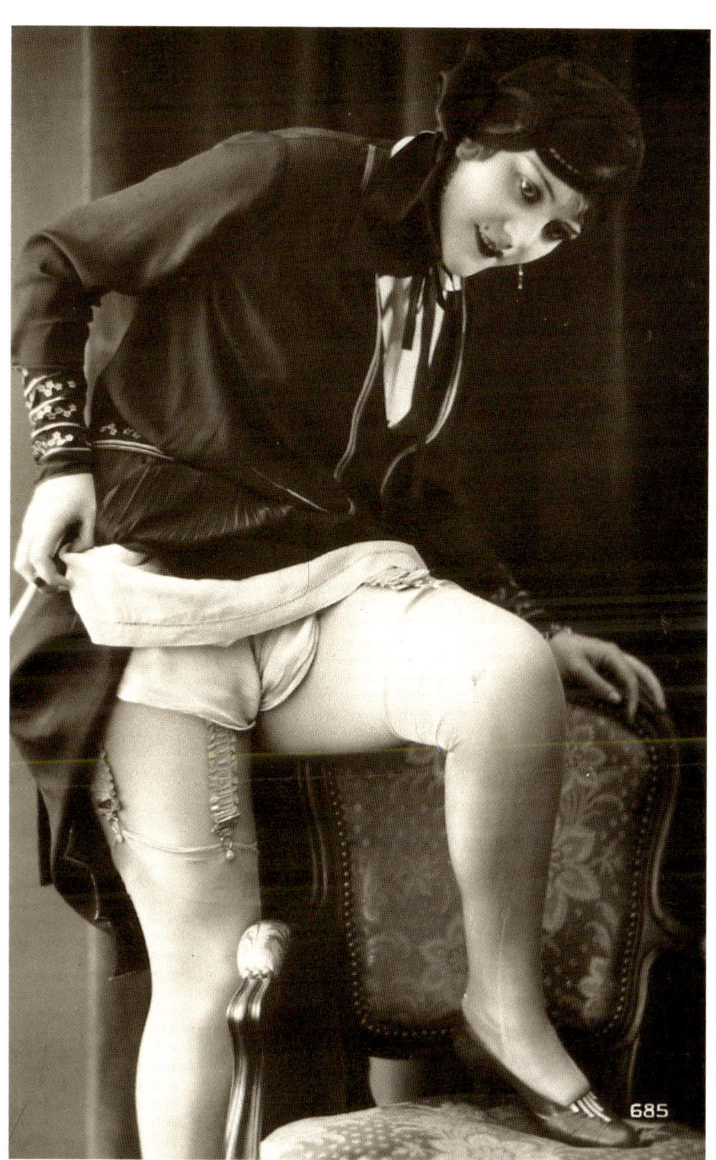
685

I am not a woman – I am a world.
My garments only have to fall
and on my body you will find
a whole series of secrets.

Gustave Flaubert

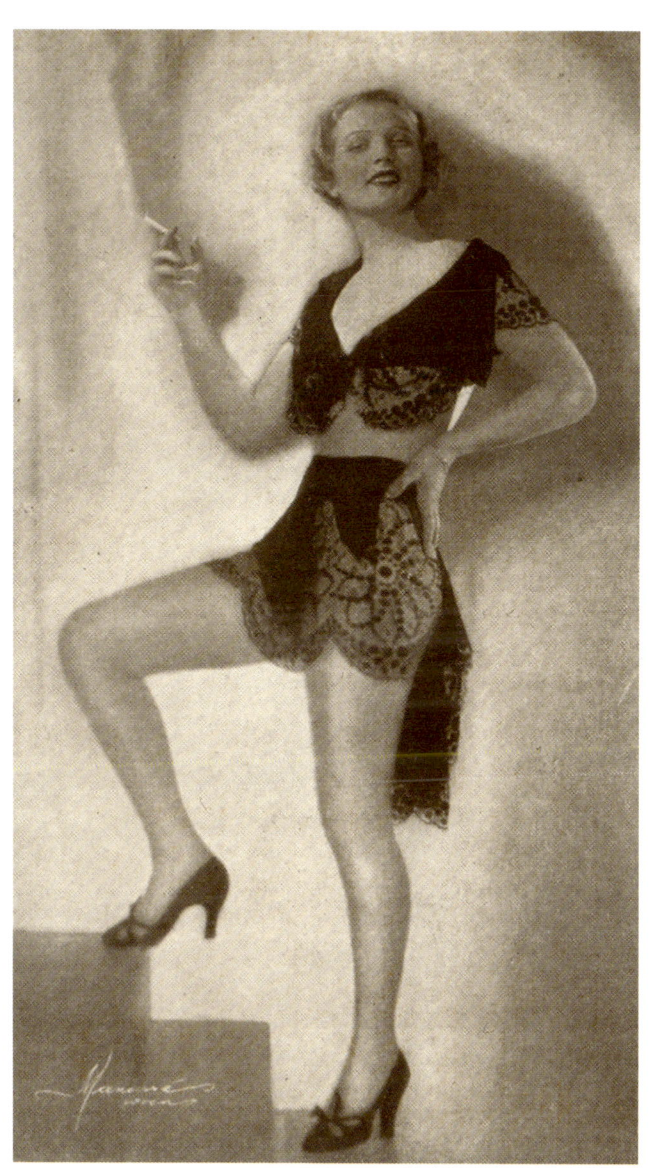

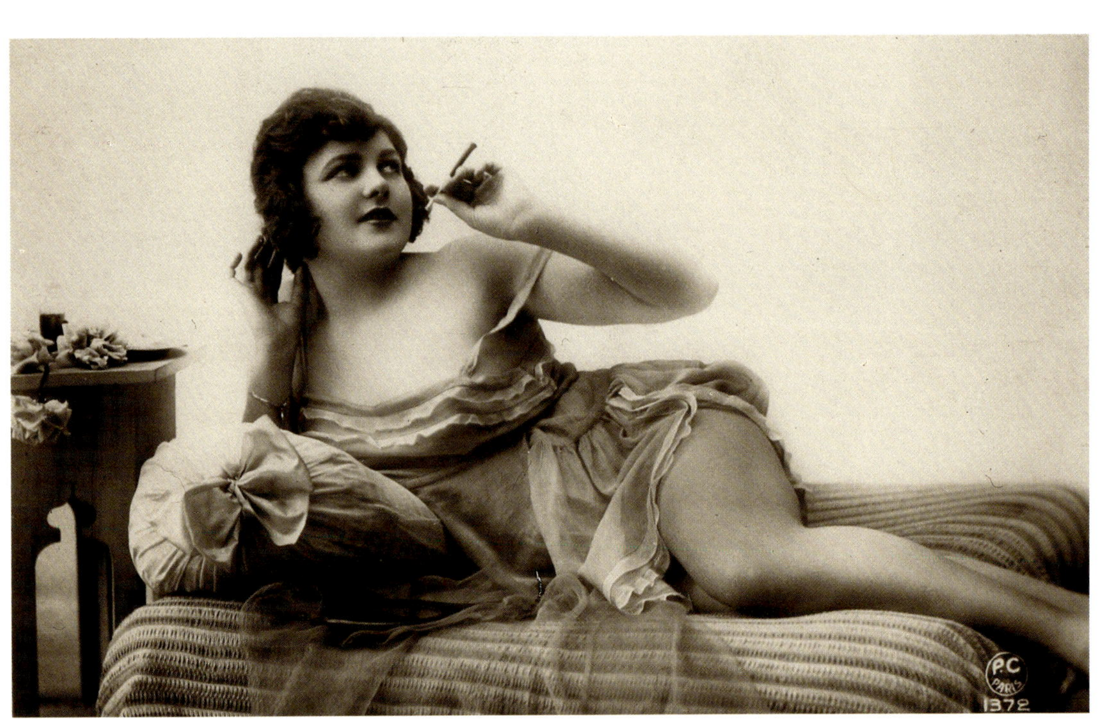
P.C
PARIS
1372

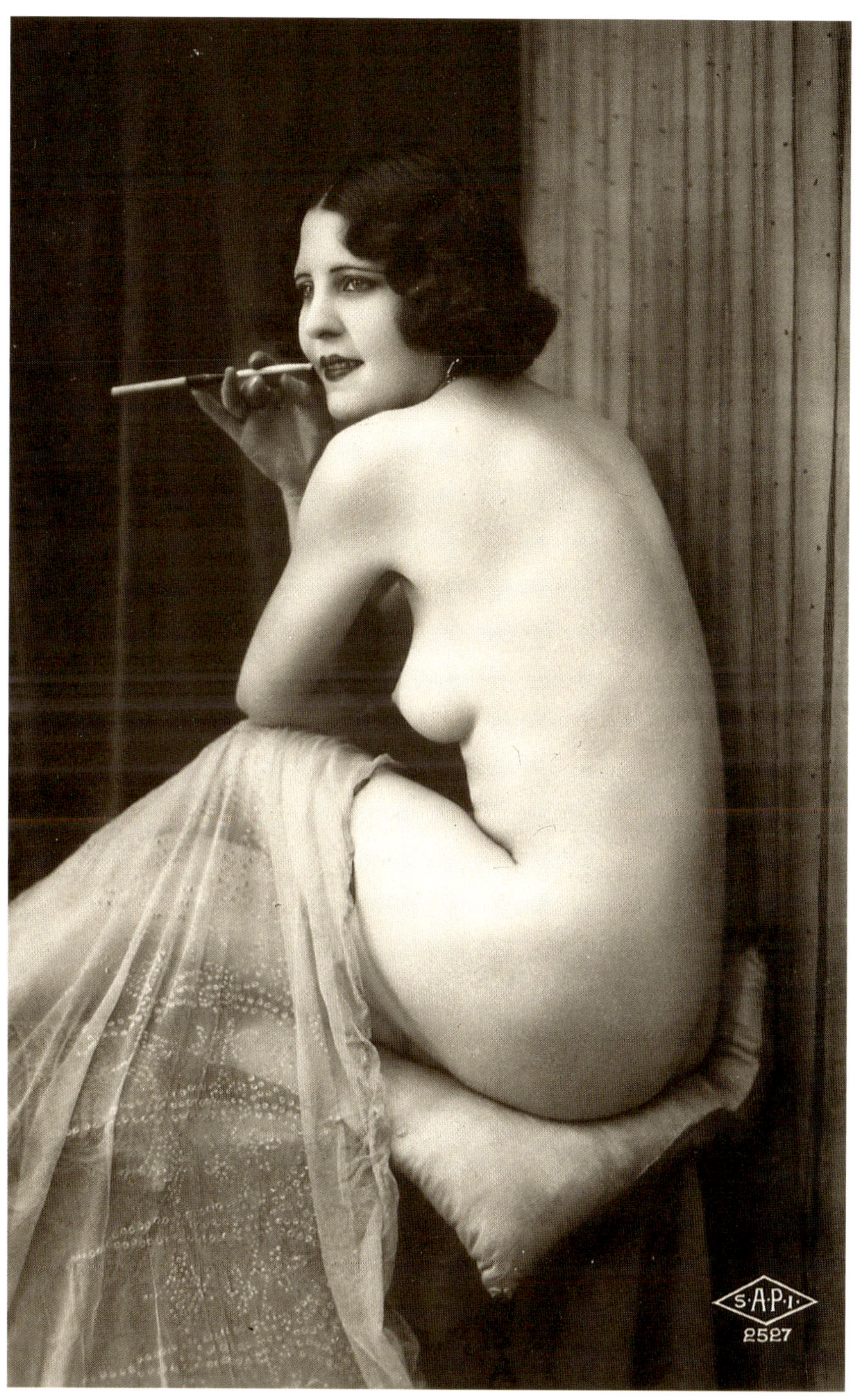
S·A·P·I·
2527

Daily we see so many fools being caught in a pretty woman's net and being made the toy of her wickedness.

La Fontaine

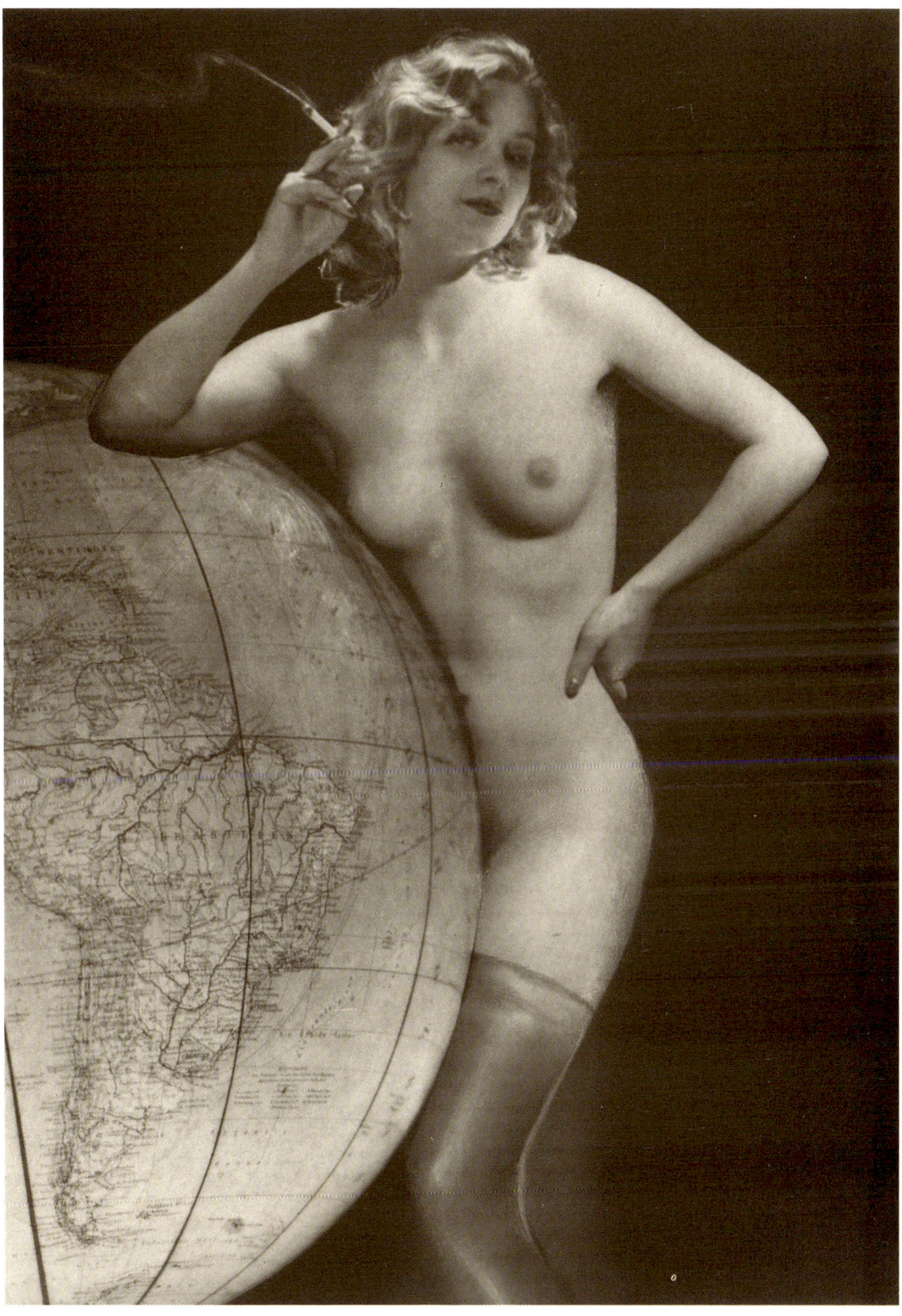

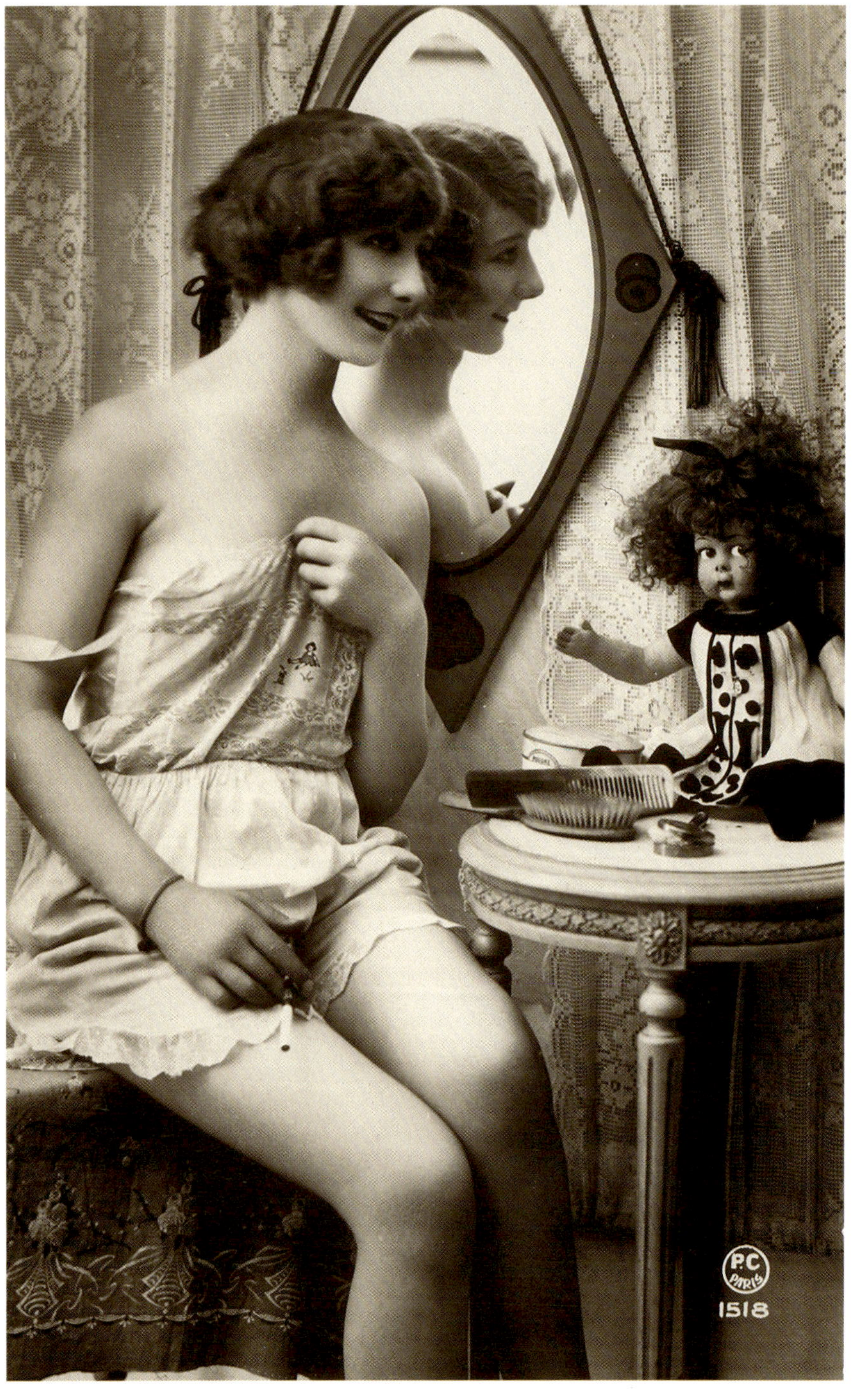
P.C
PARIS
1518

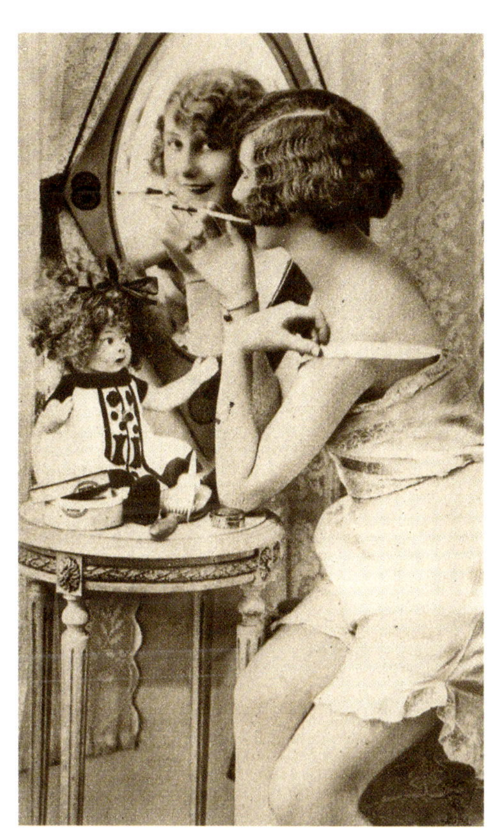

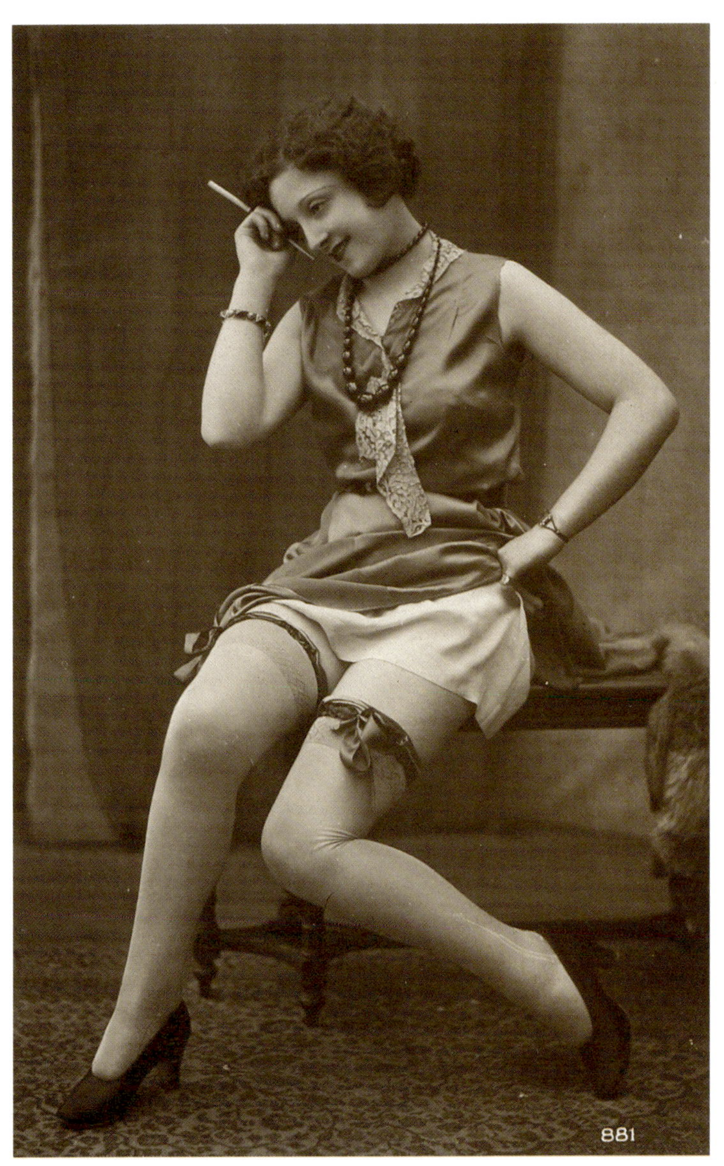
881

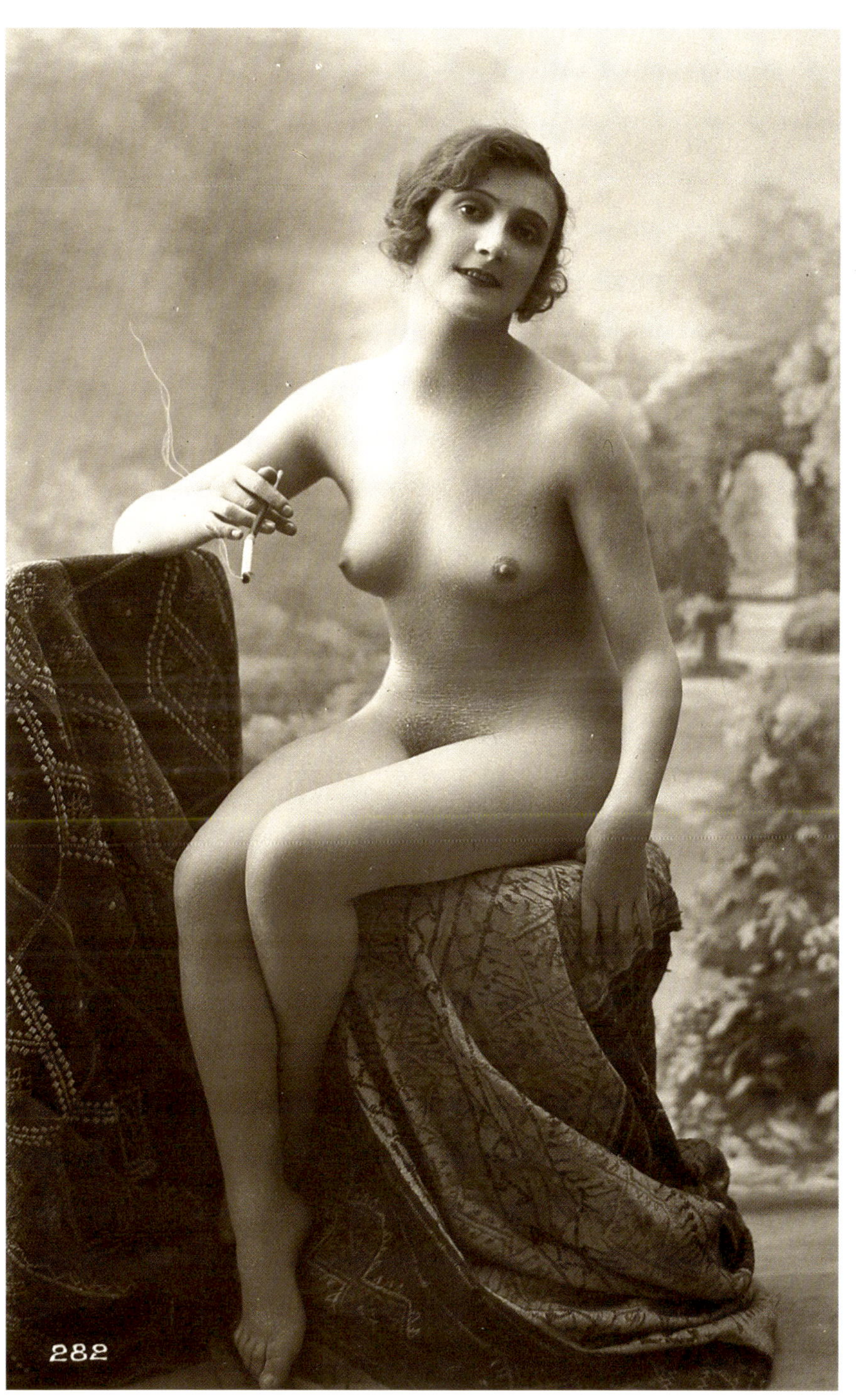
282

Love,
you alone create my misfortune.

Pierre de Ronsard

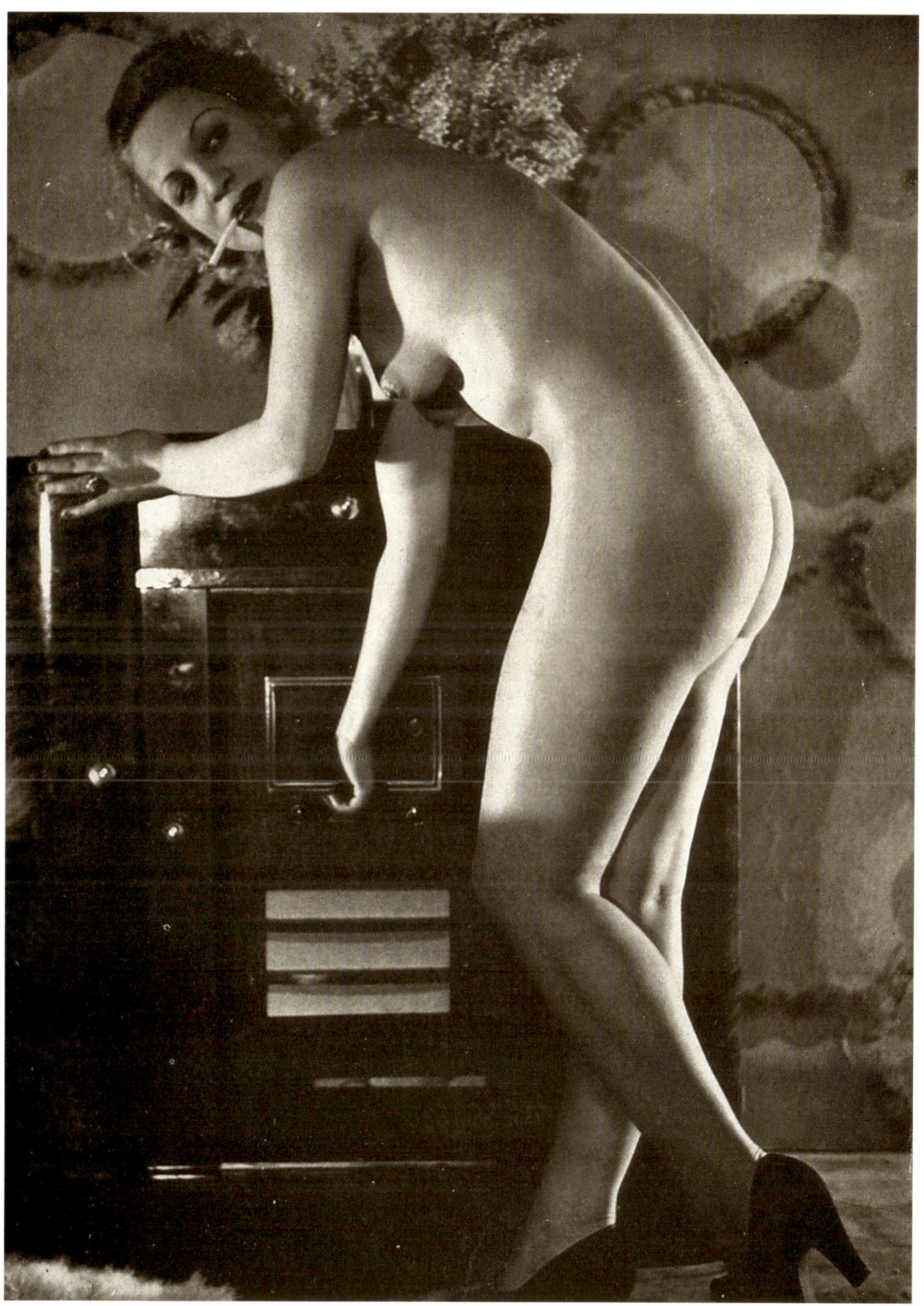

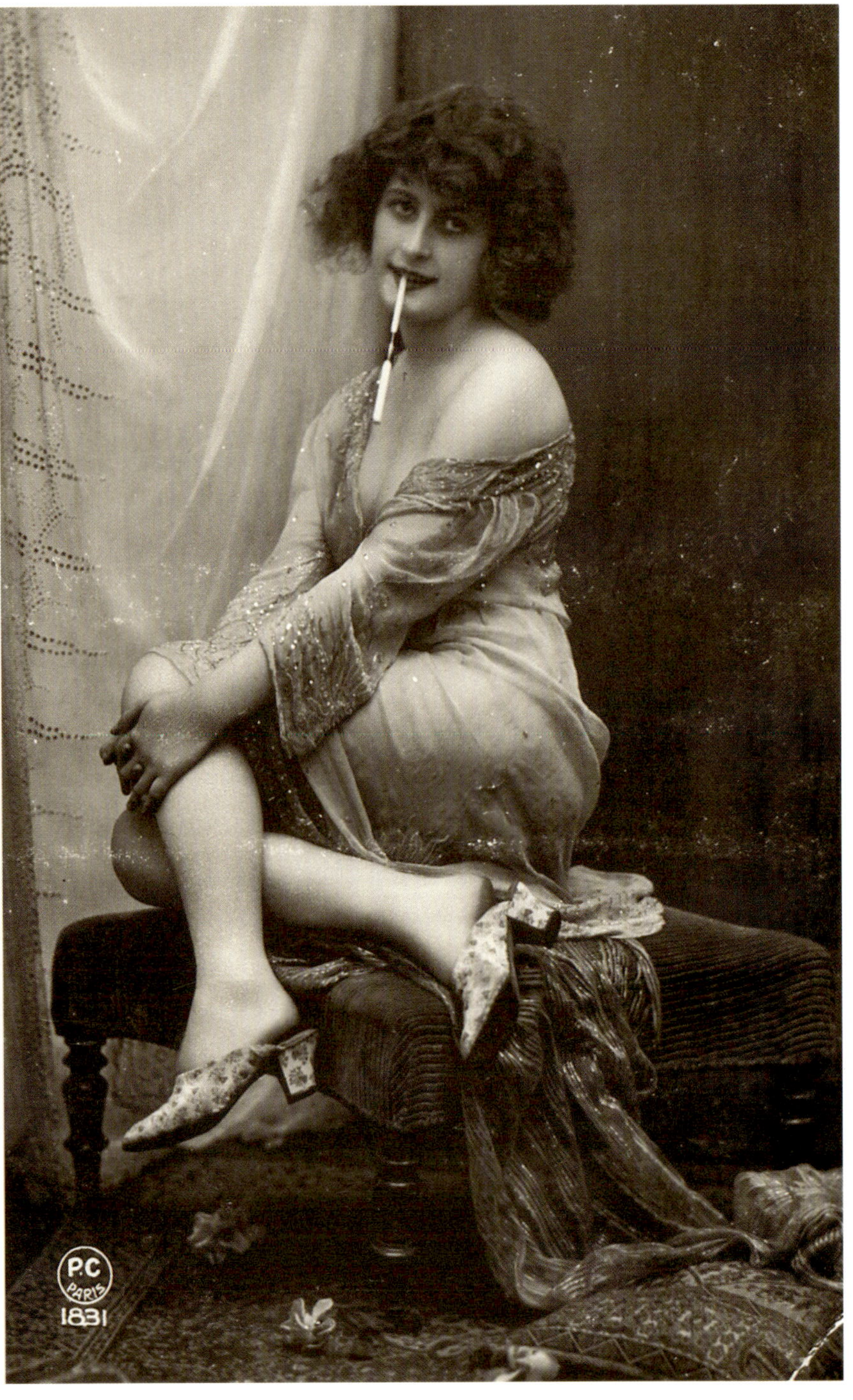
P.C
PARIS
1831

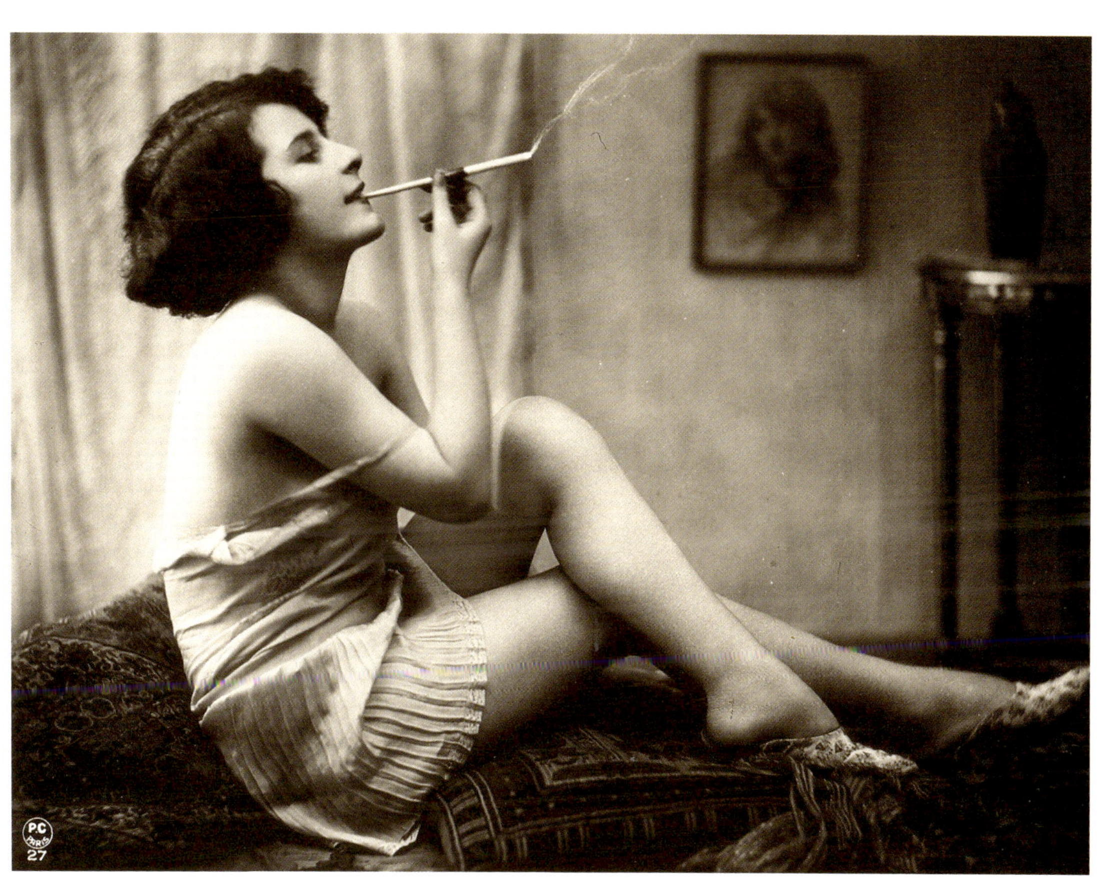
P.C
PARIS
27

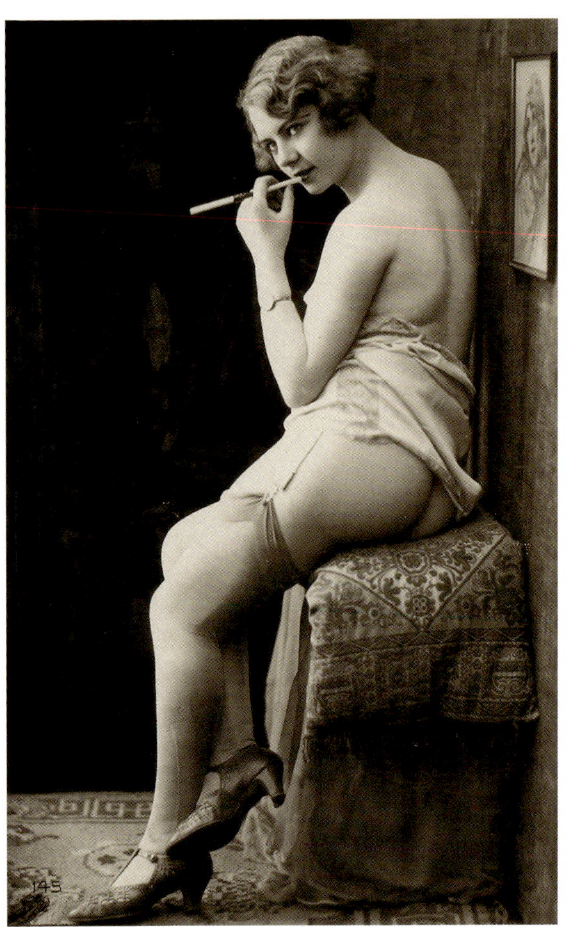
145

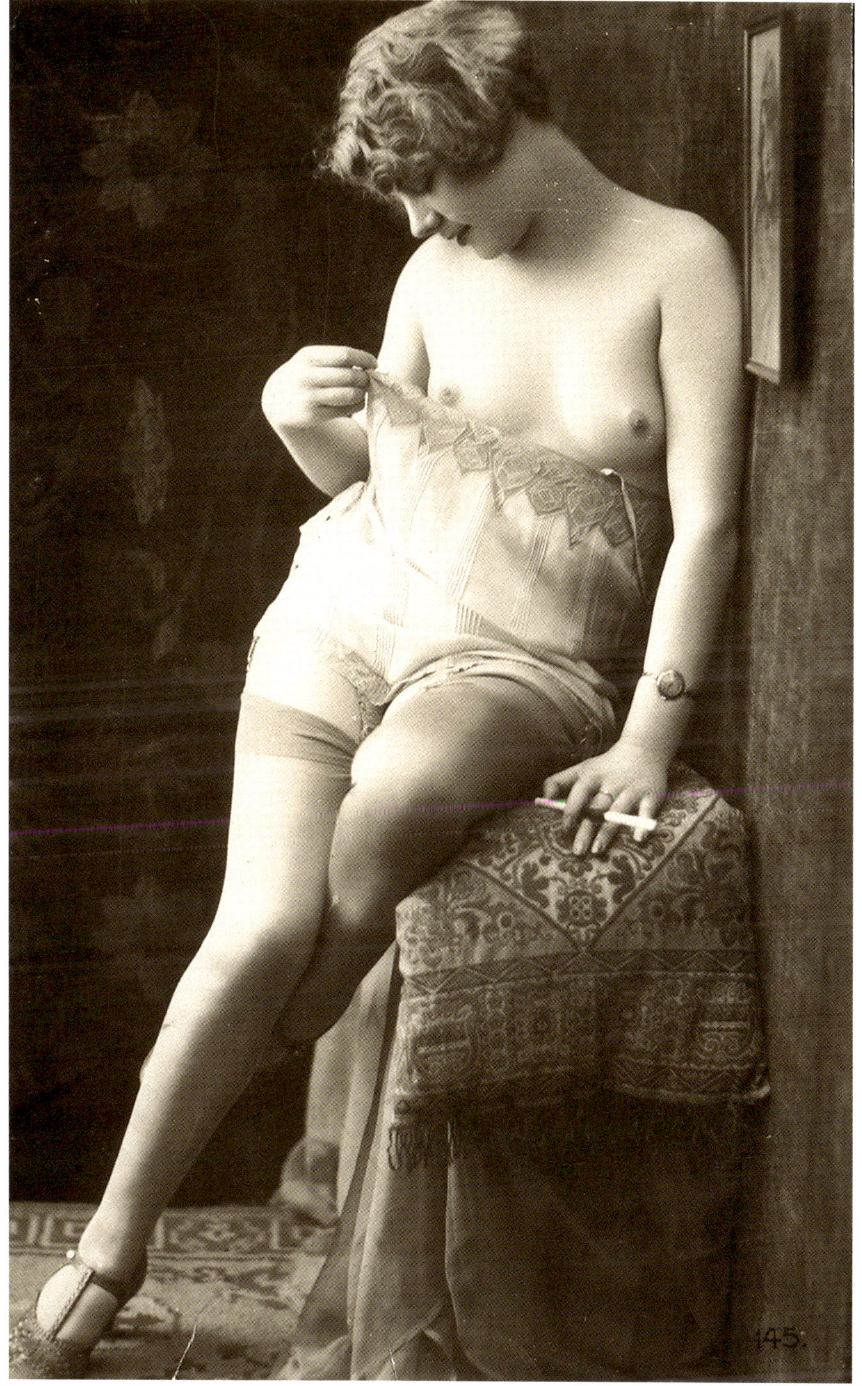
145.

There are women who say:
"For you I am ruining myself !"
Others say: "You will despise me."
These are only different ways of expressing the
fatality of love. But she, she did not speak one word.

Barbey d'Aurevilly

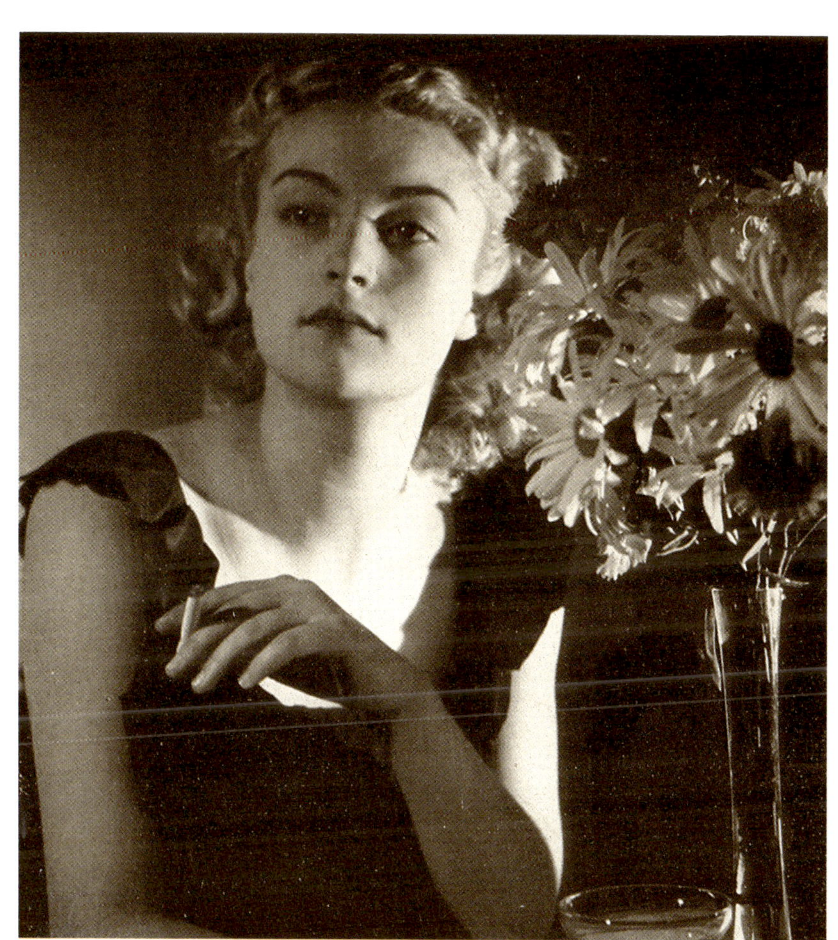

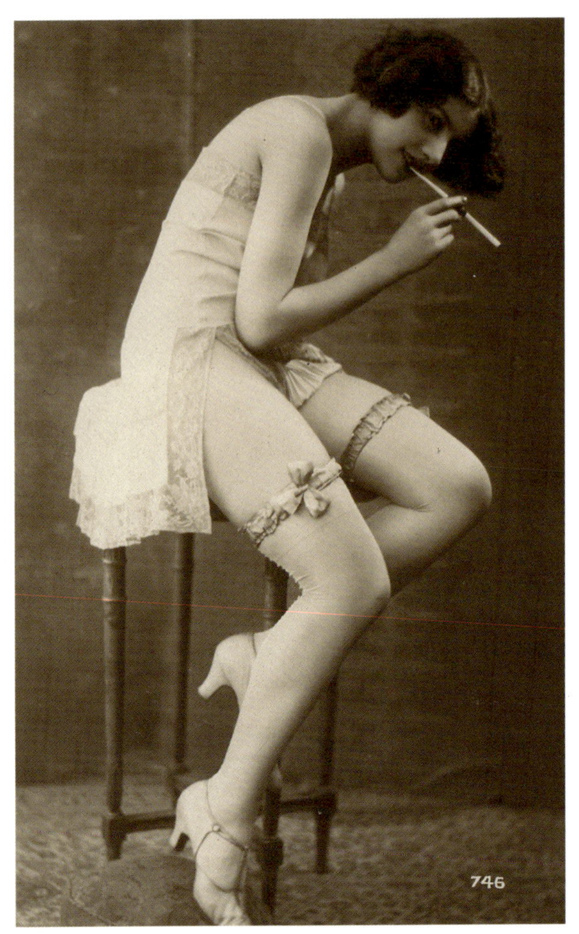
746

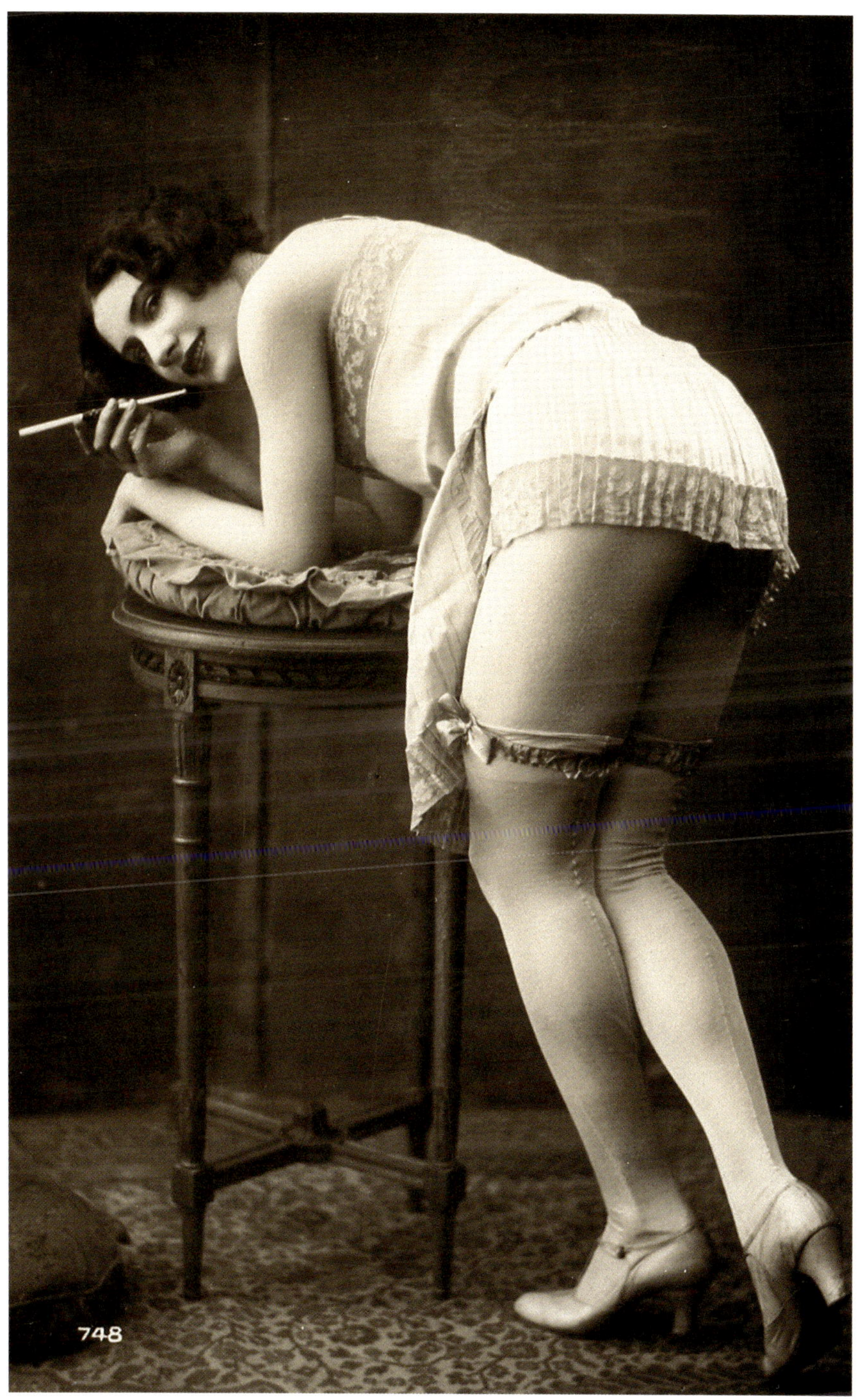
748

She was not quite naked
but this was much worse! She was far more indecent,
much more shockingly indecent this way
than if she had been simply naked.
Marble statues are naked and their nakedness is chaste.
This is the bravery of chastity.

Barbey d'Aurevilly

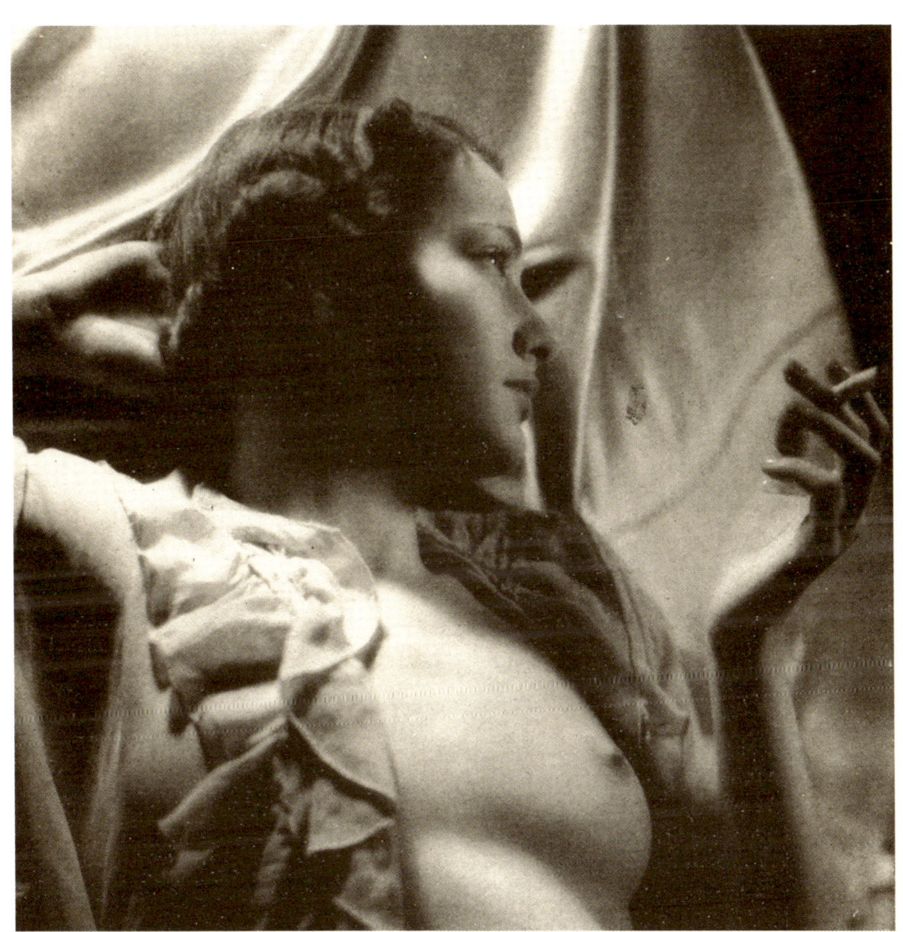

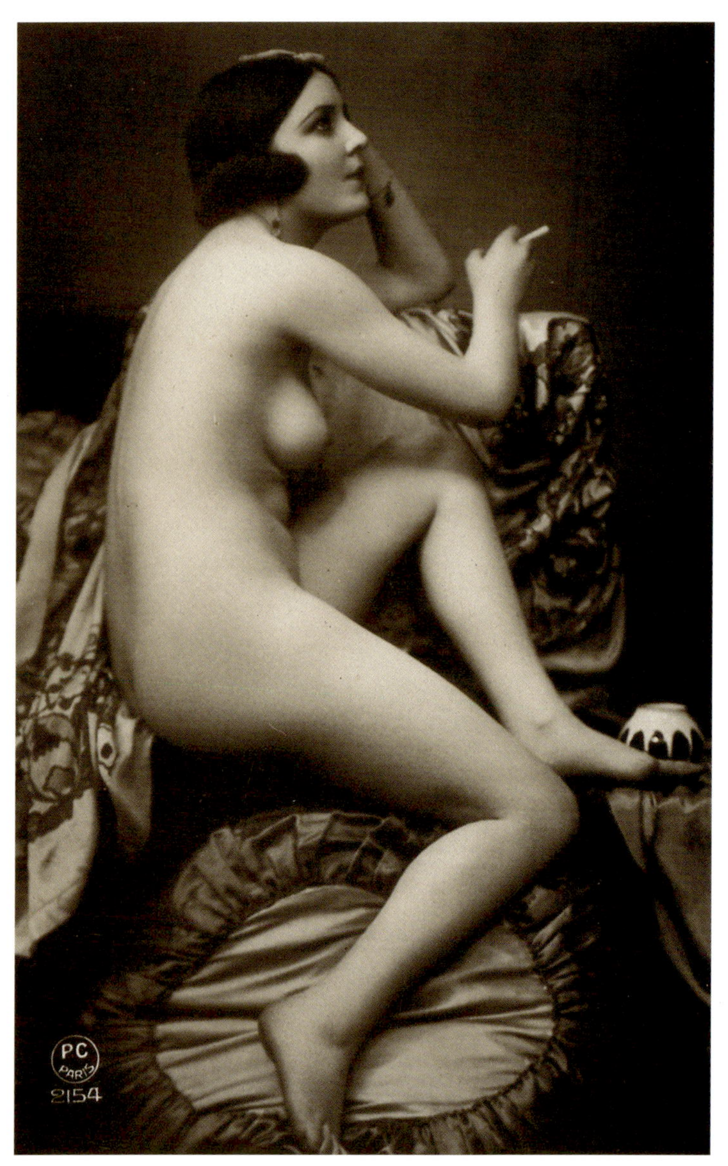
PC
PARIS
2154

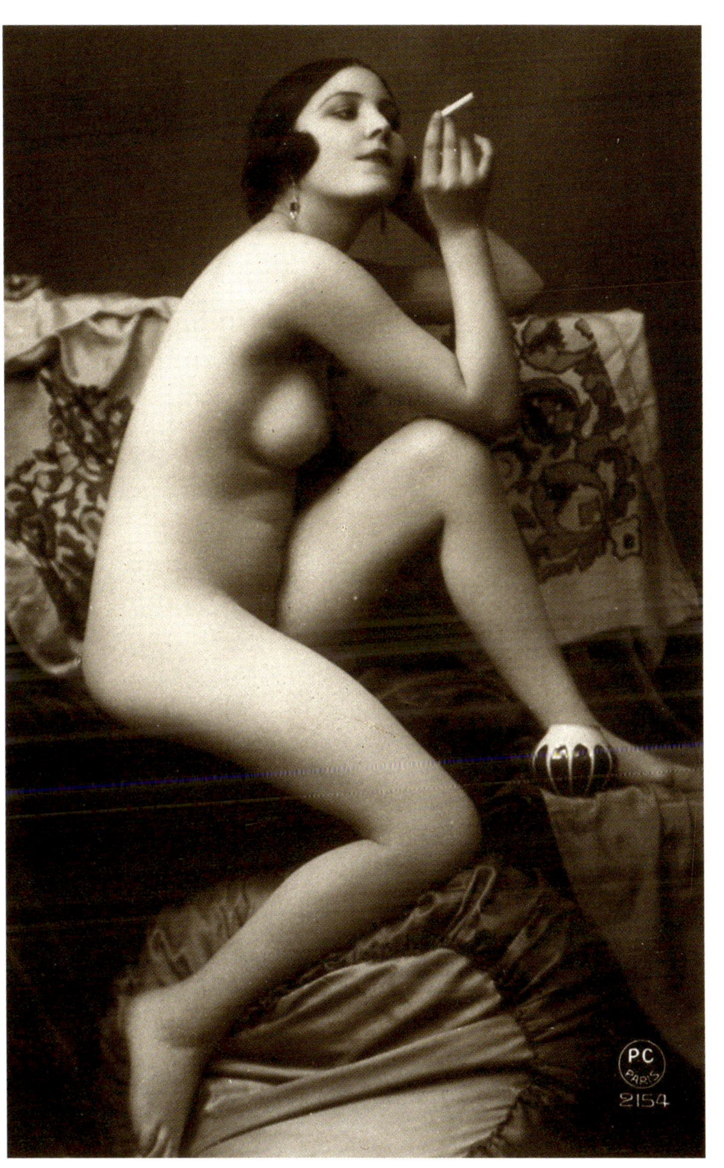
PC
PARIS
2154

The important event in love is the moment when nakedness is revealed.

Pierre Louÿs

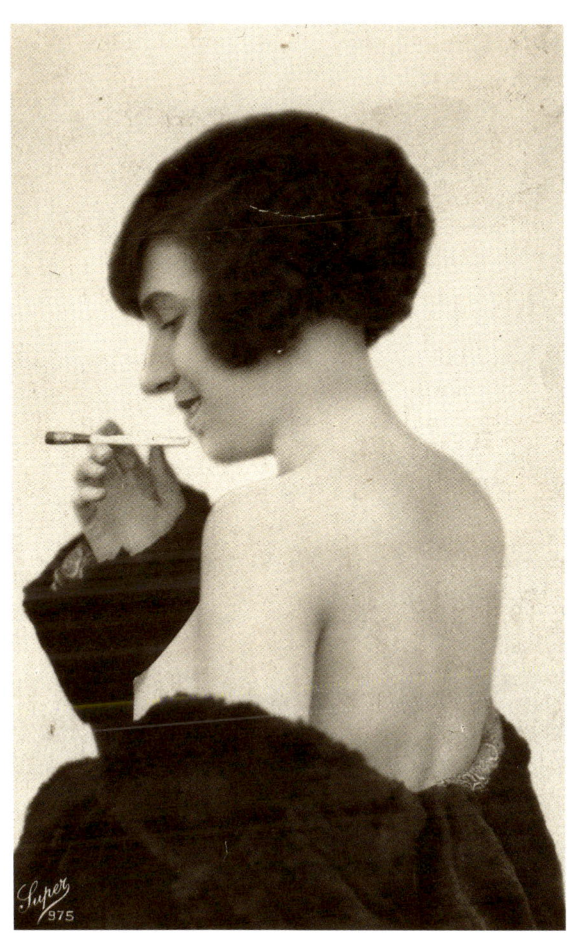
Super
975

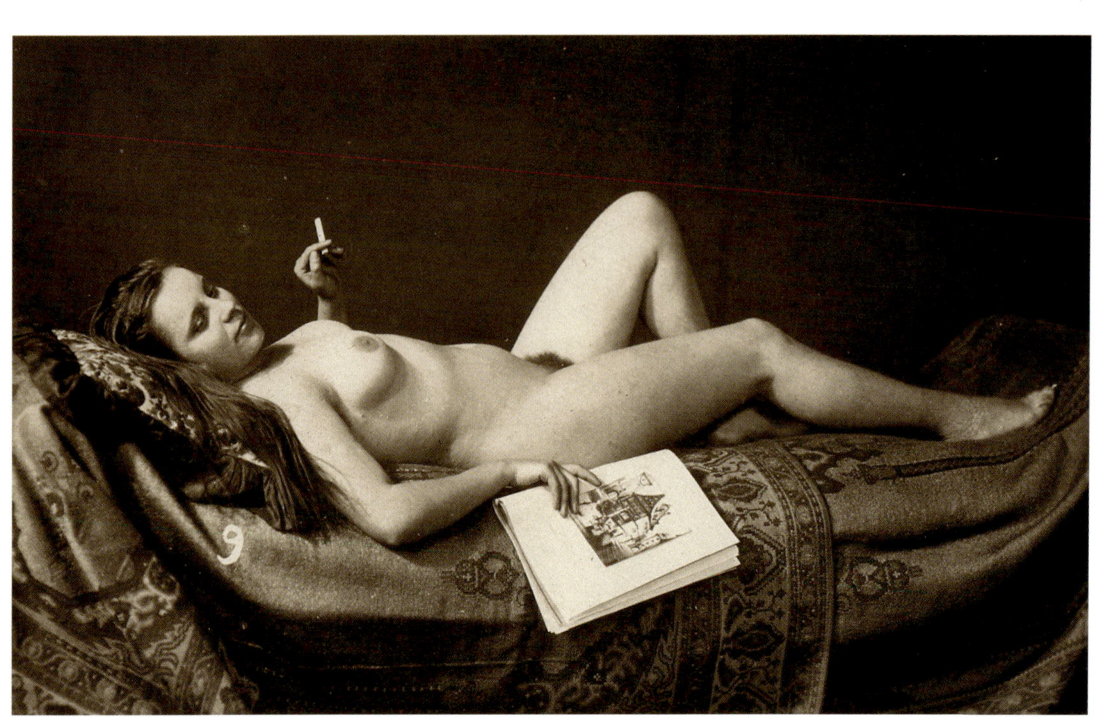

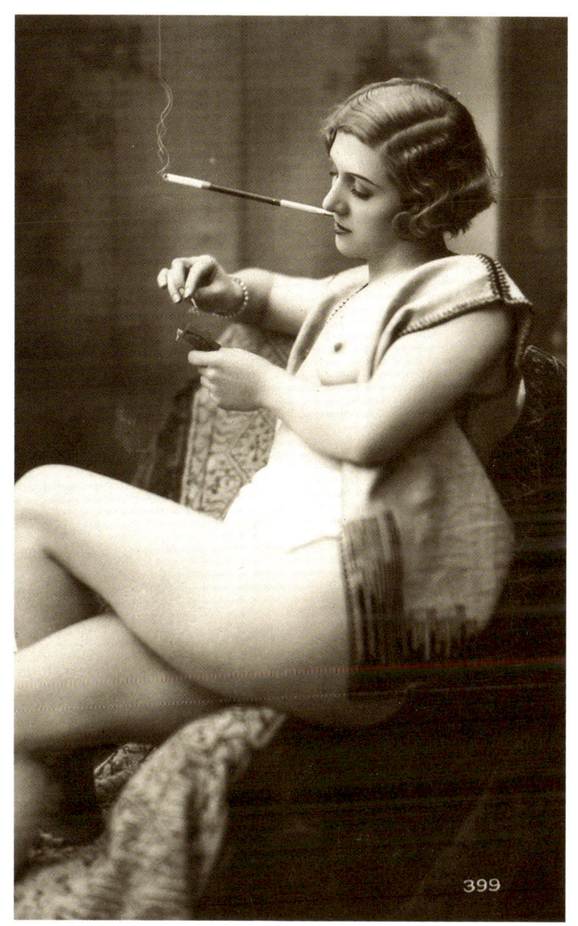
399

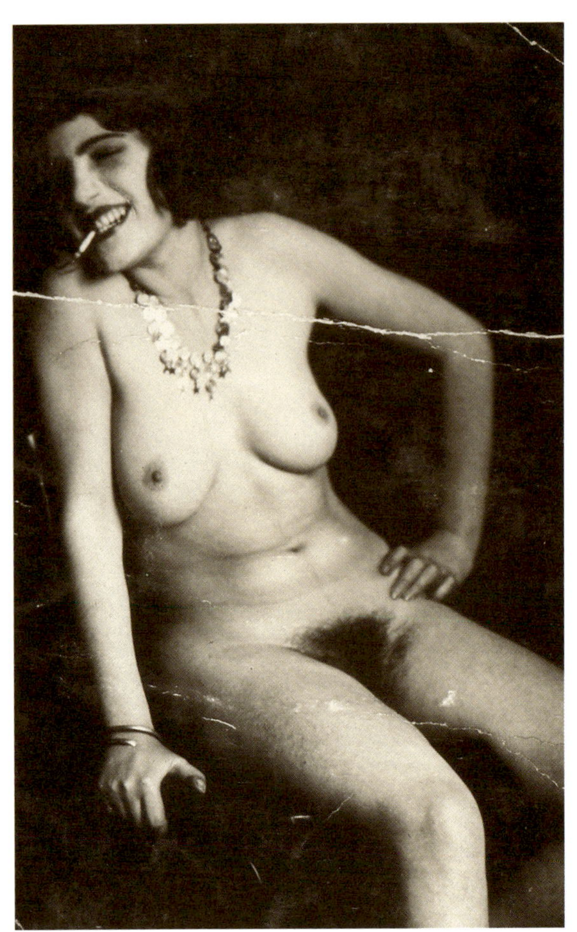

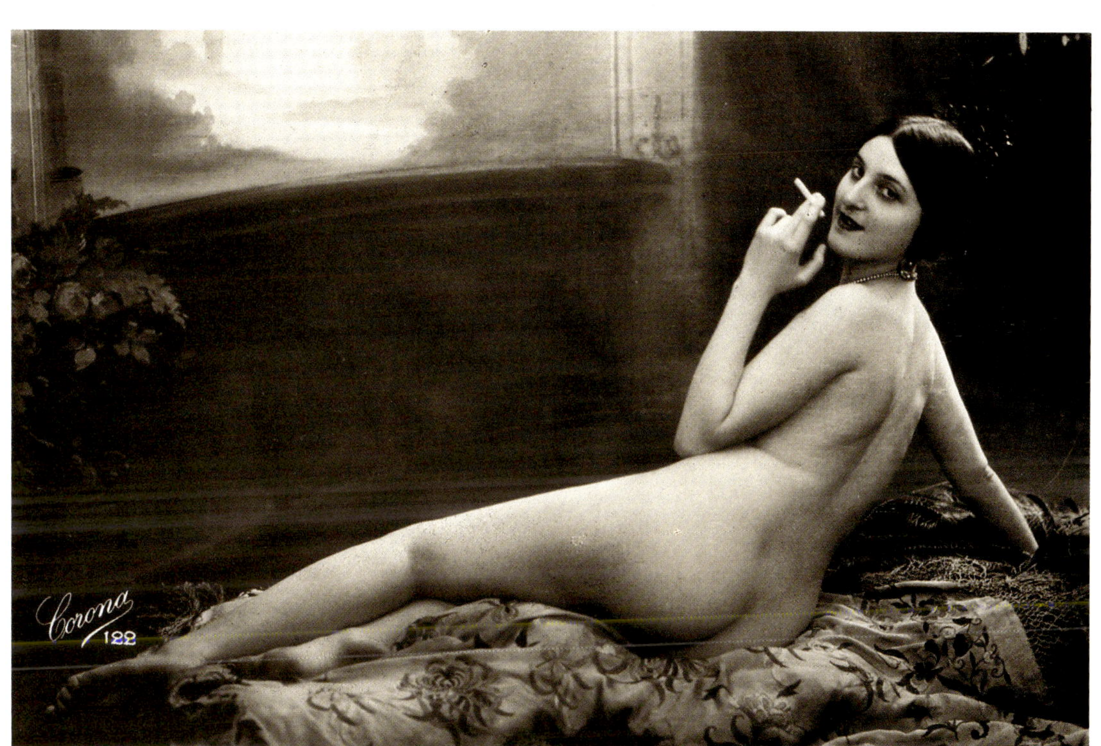
Corona
122

As a lady said to her lover:
"You find the ways and means of letting me feel lust
and I shall easily find out how to satisfy my desire."

Seigneur de Brantôme

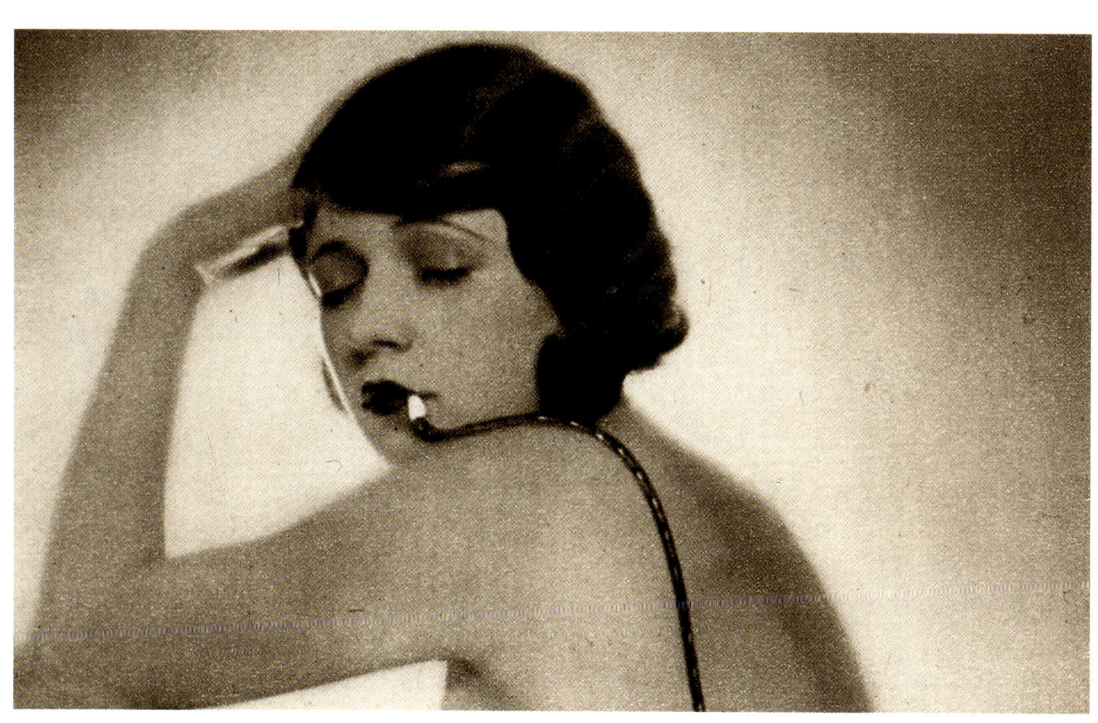

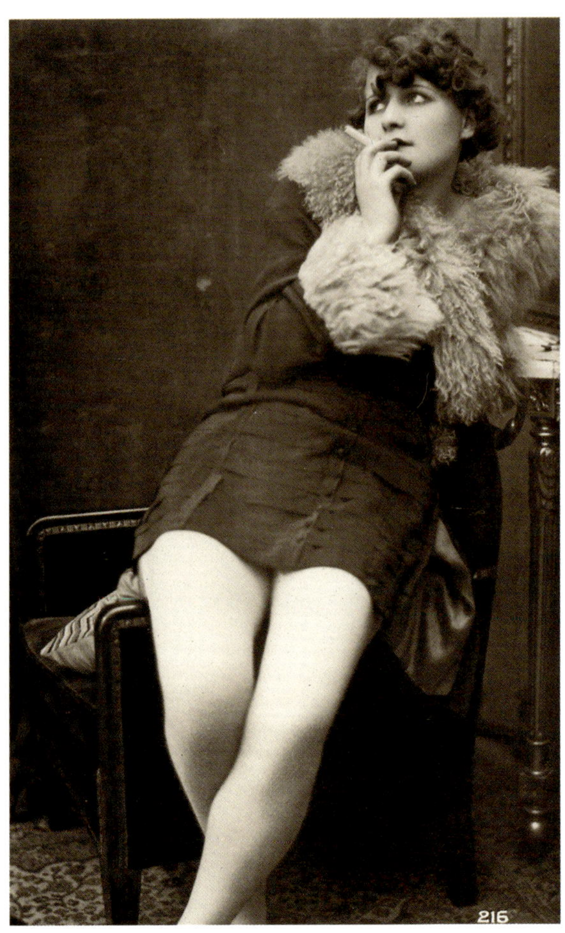
216

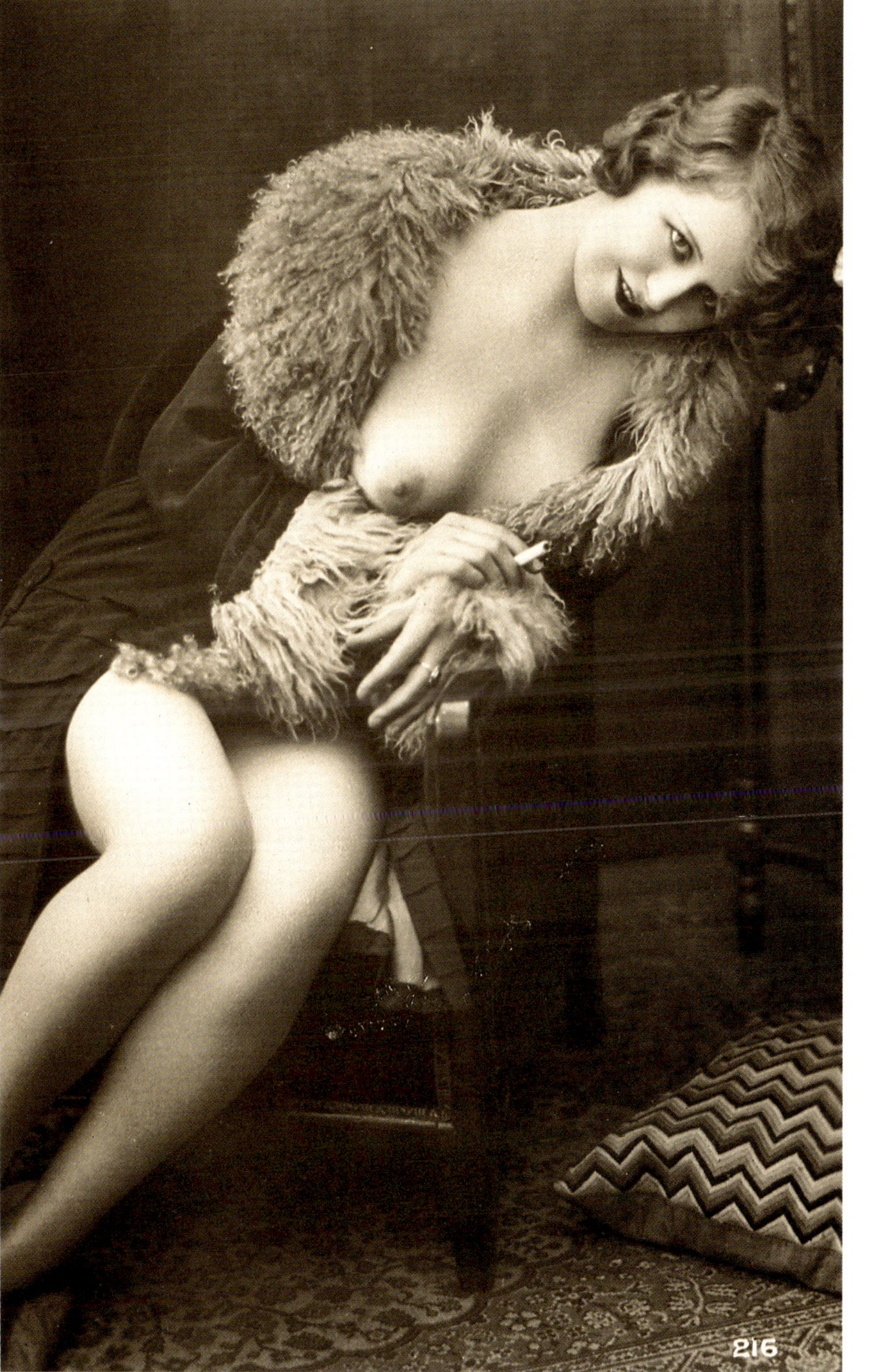
216

As long as he was strong enough to walk
he went again and
again to this cursed woman,
who took all his savings.

Honoré de Balzac

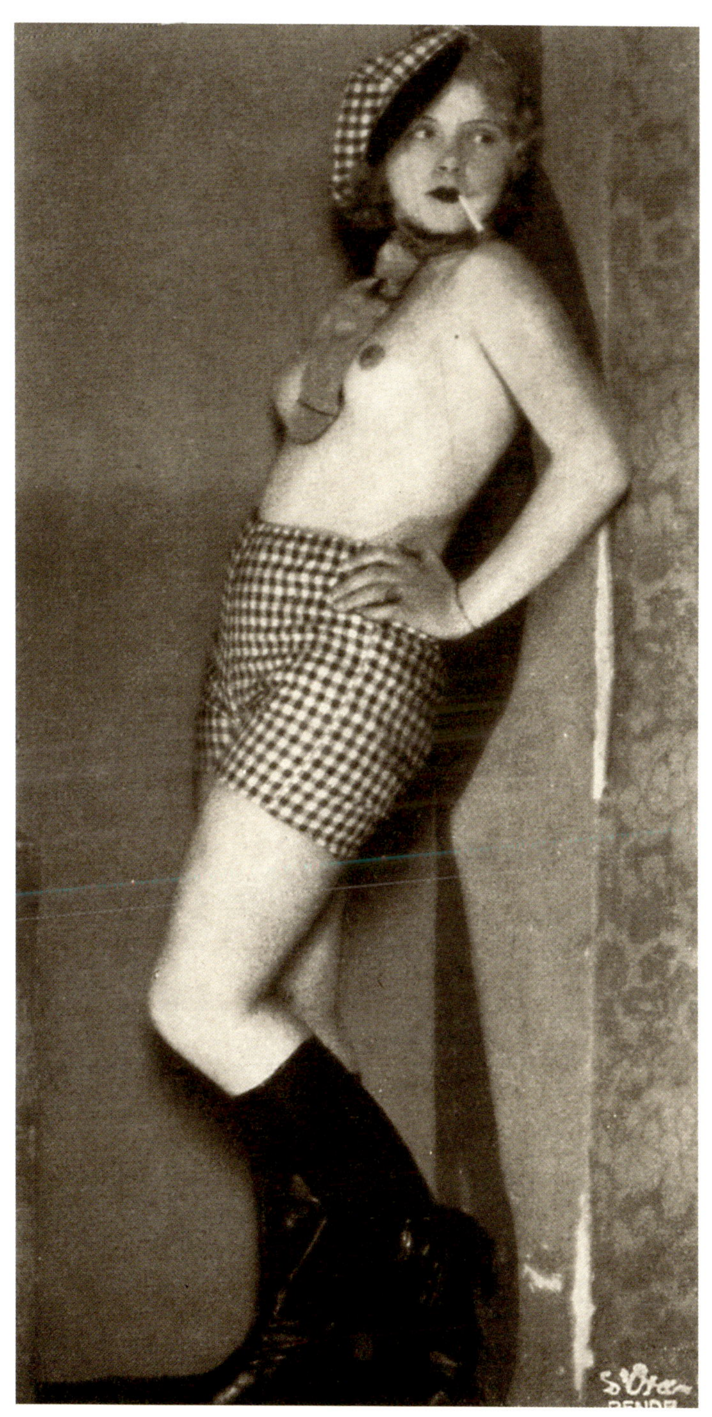
d'Ora

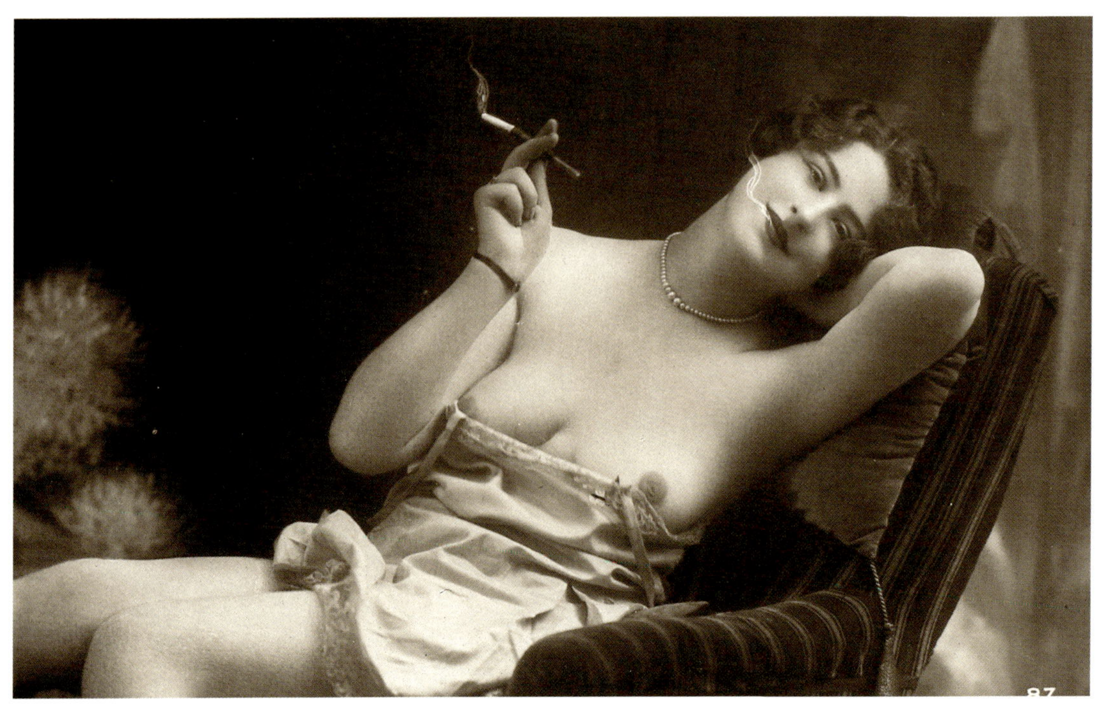

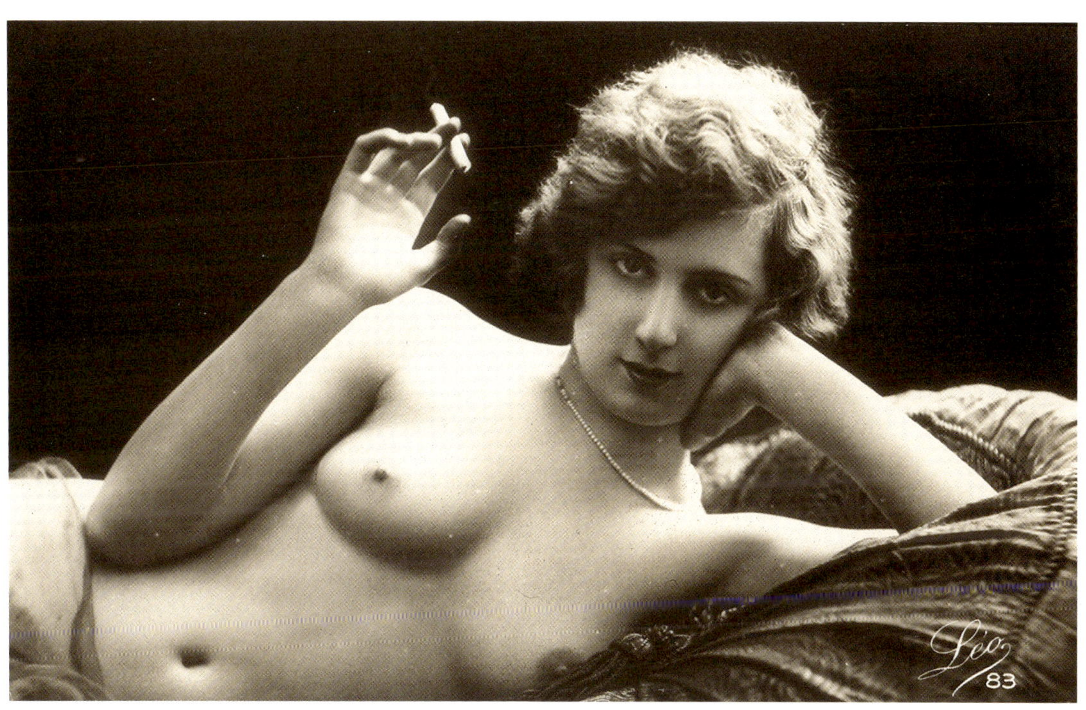
Léo
83

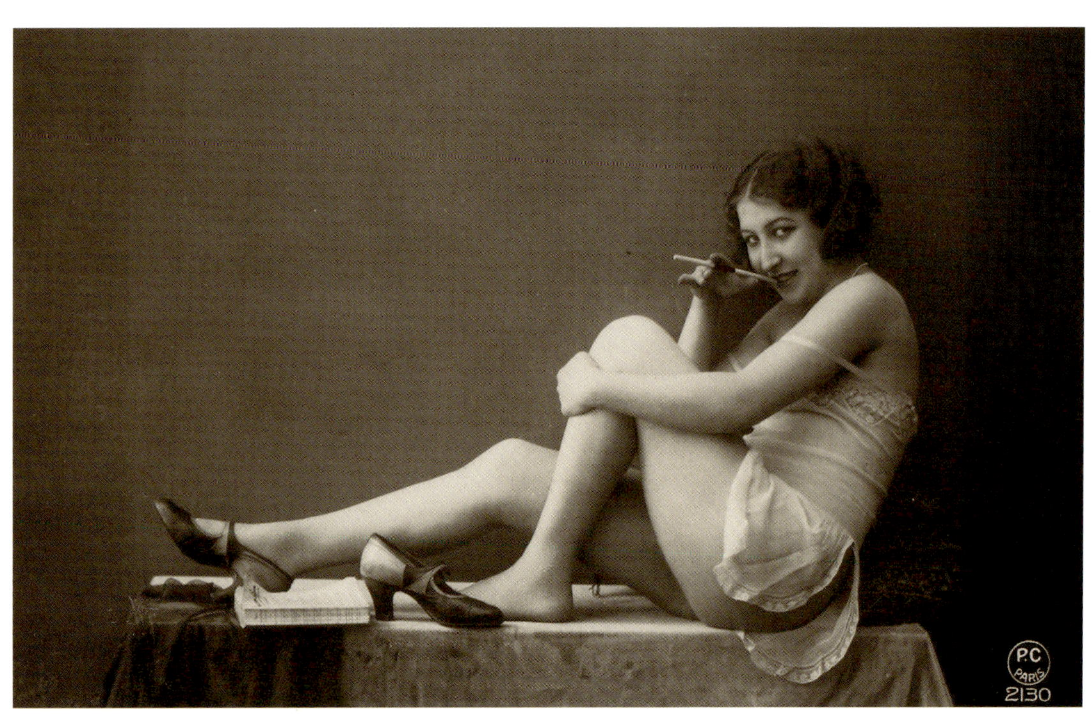
P.C
PARIS
2130

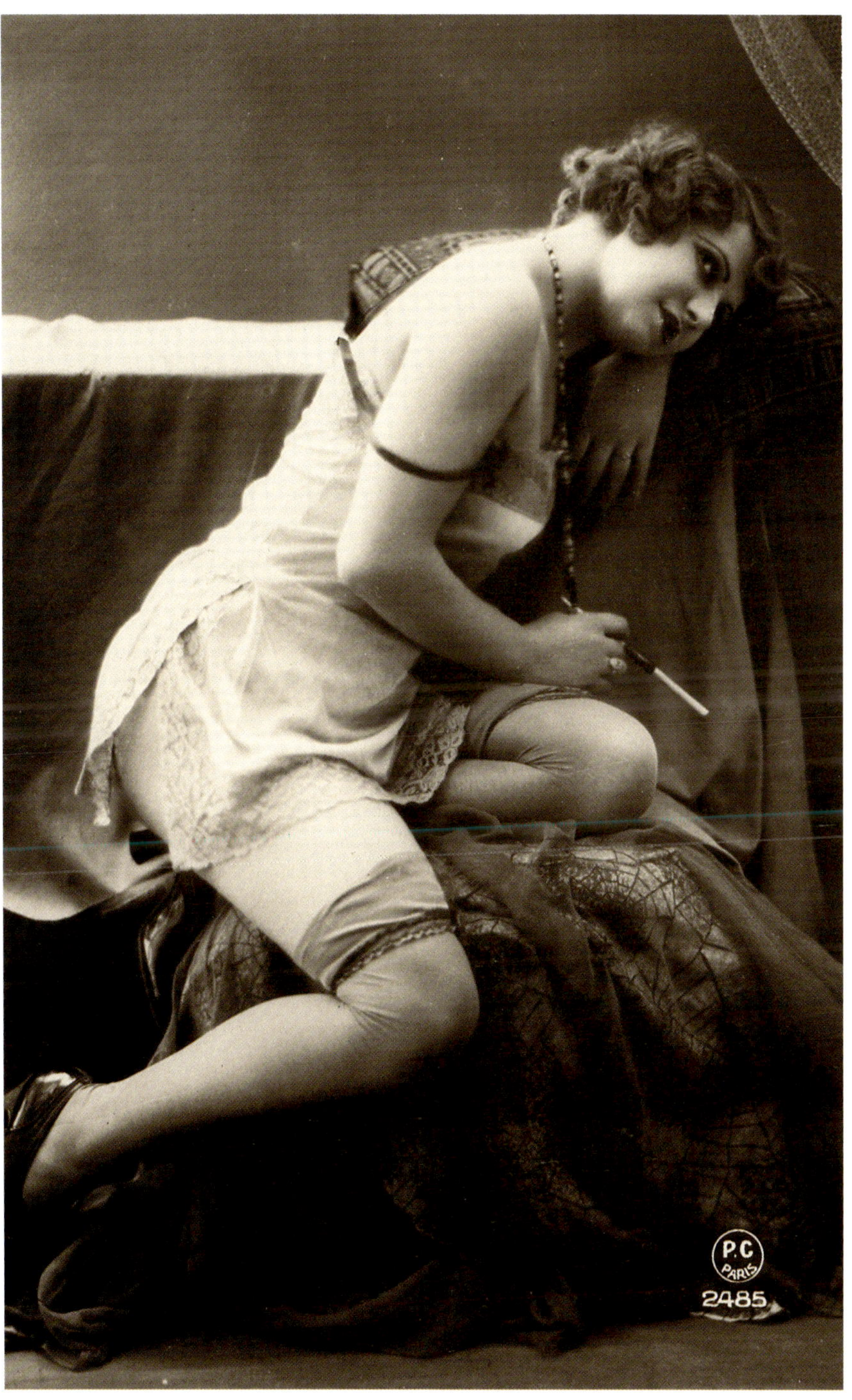
P.C
PARIS
2485

She fills my life like air, laden with the
smell of honeysuckle. And my insatiable soul
she fills with longing for eternity.

Charles Baudelaire

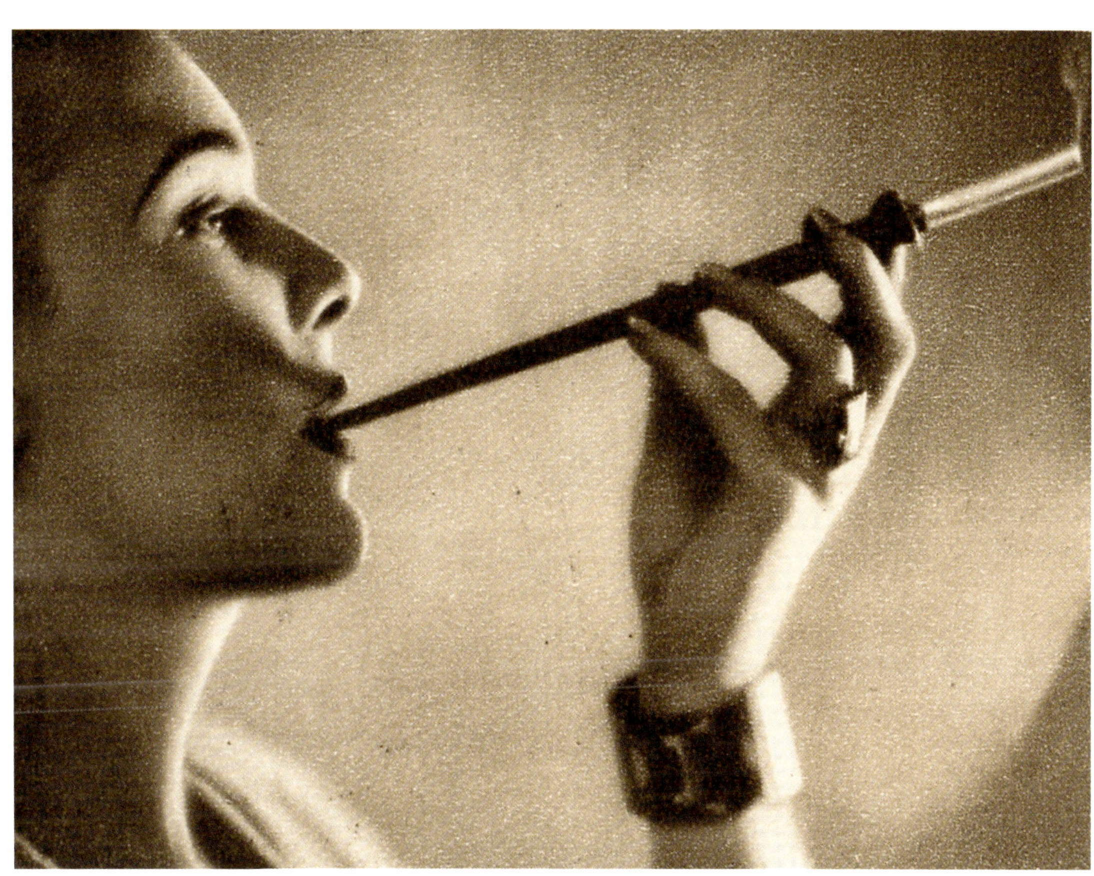

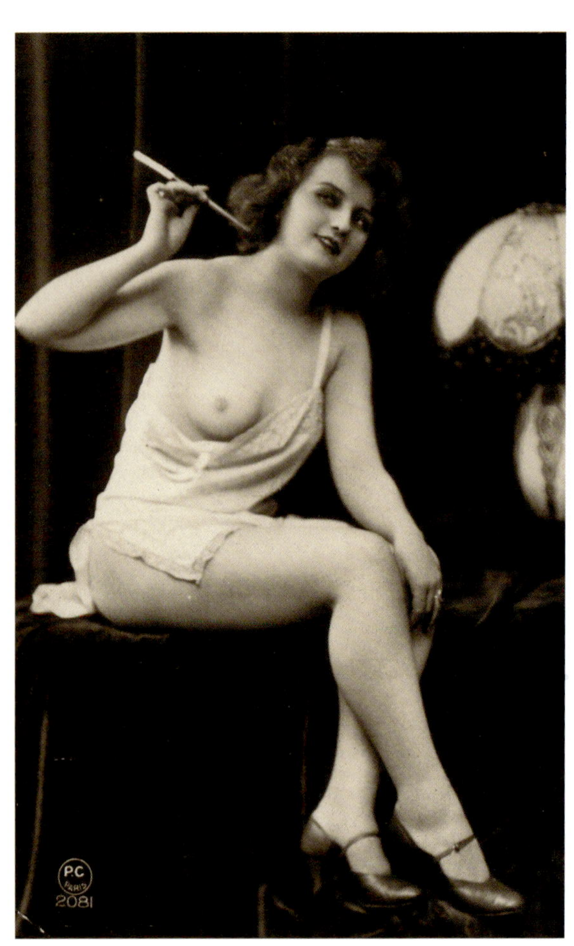
P.C
PARIS
2081

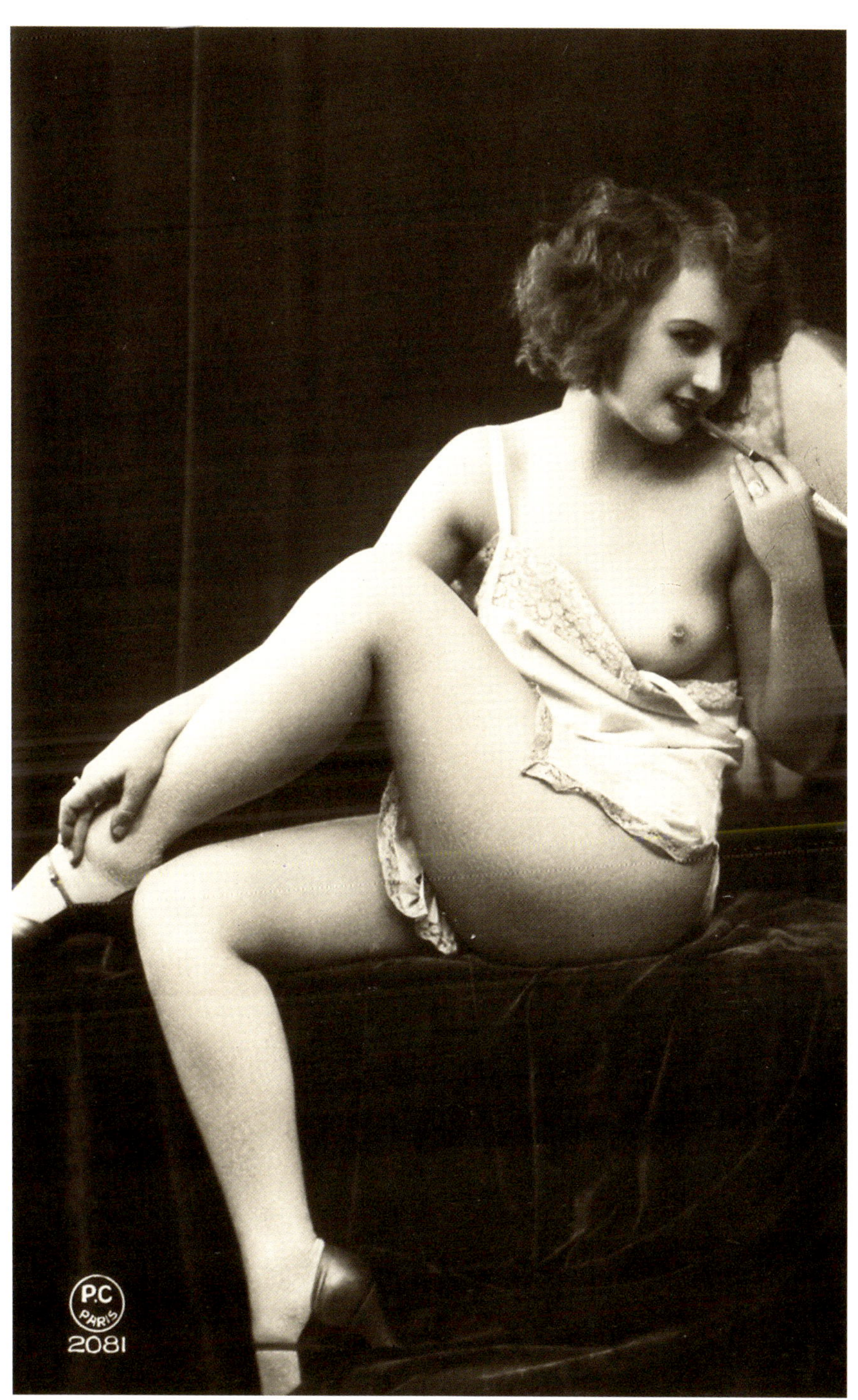
P.C
PARIS
2081

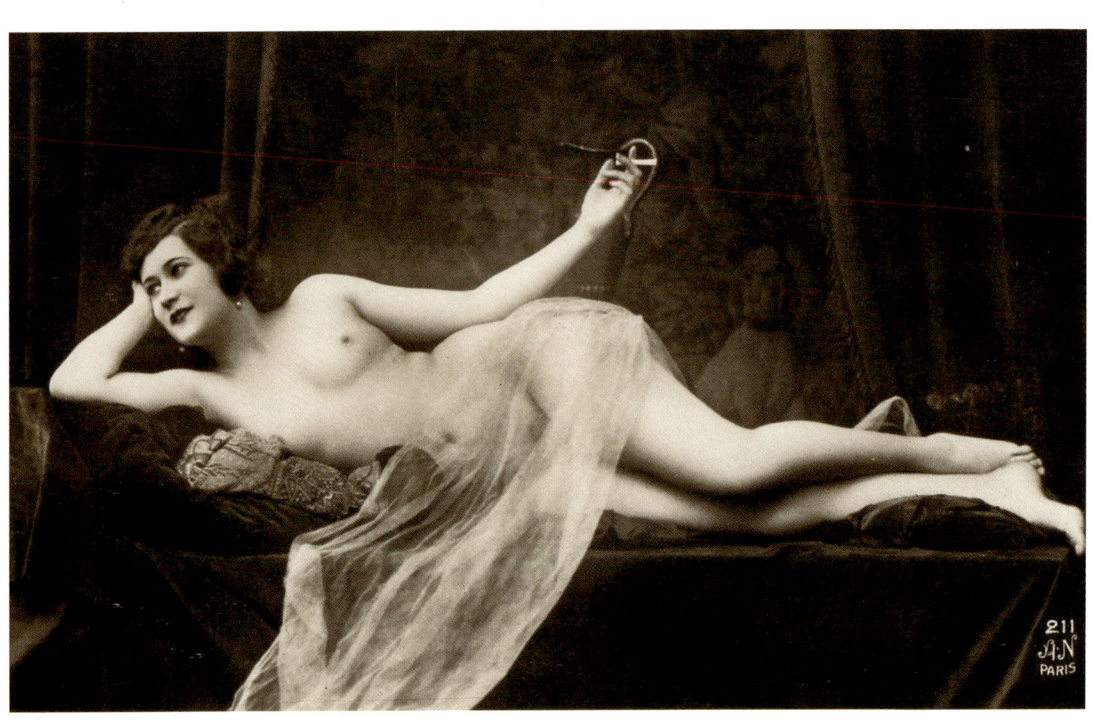
211
A·N
PARIS

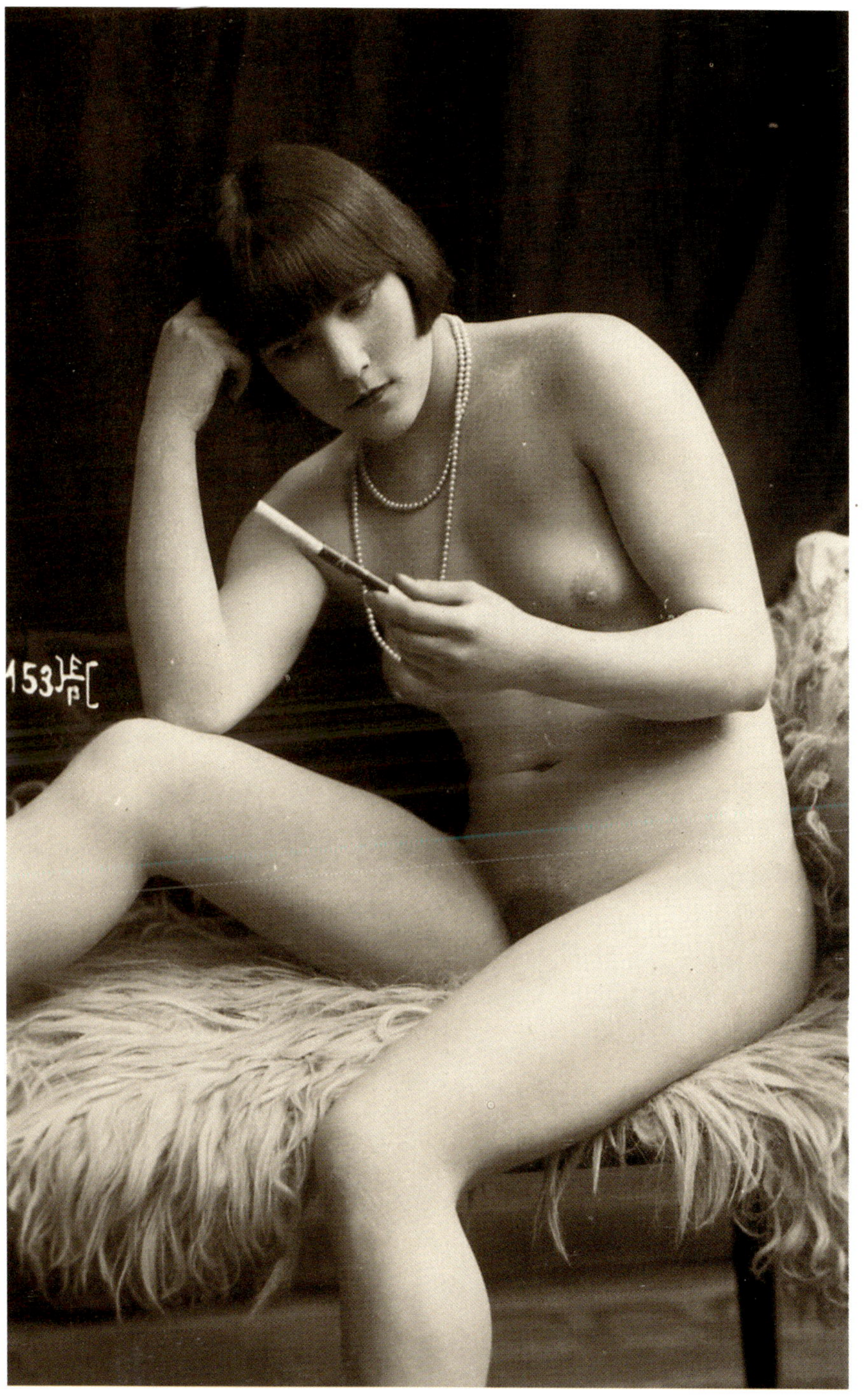

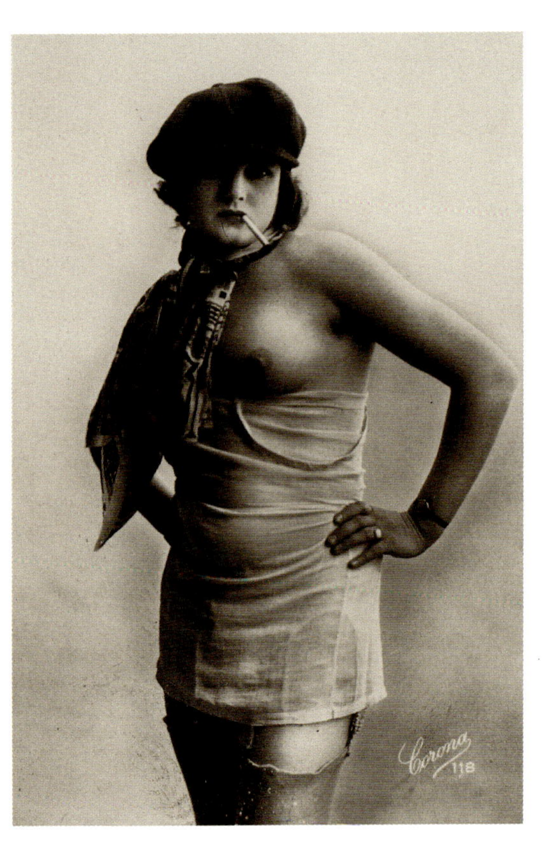
Corona
118

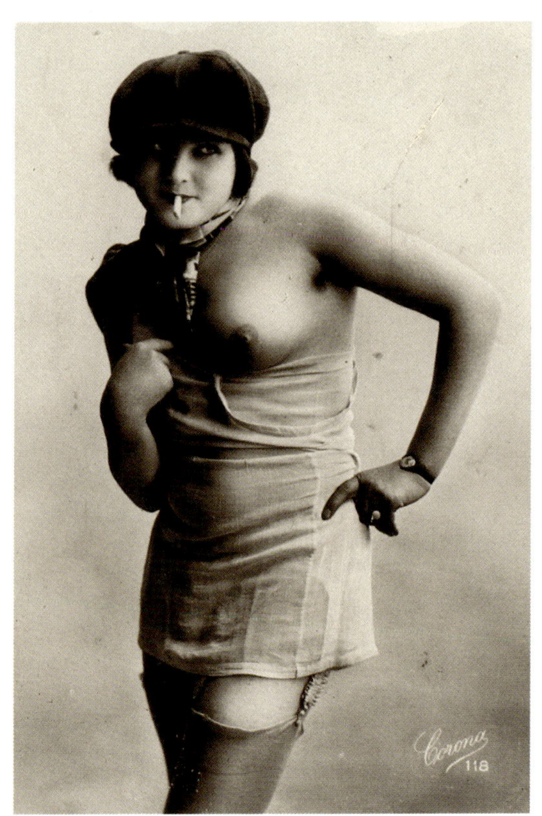
Corona
118

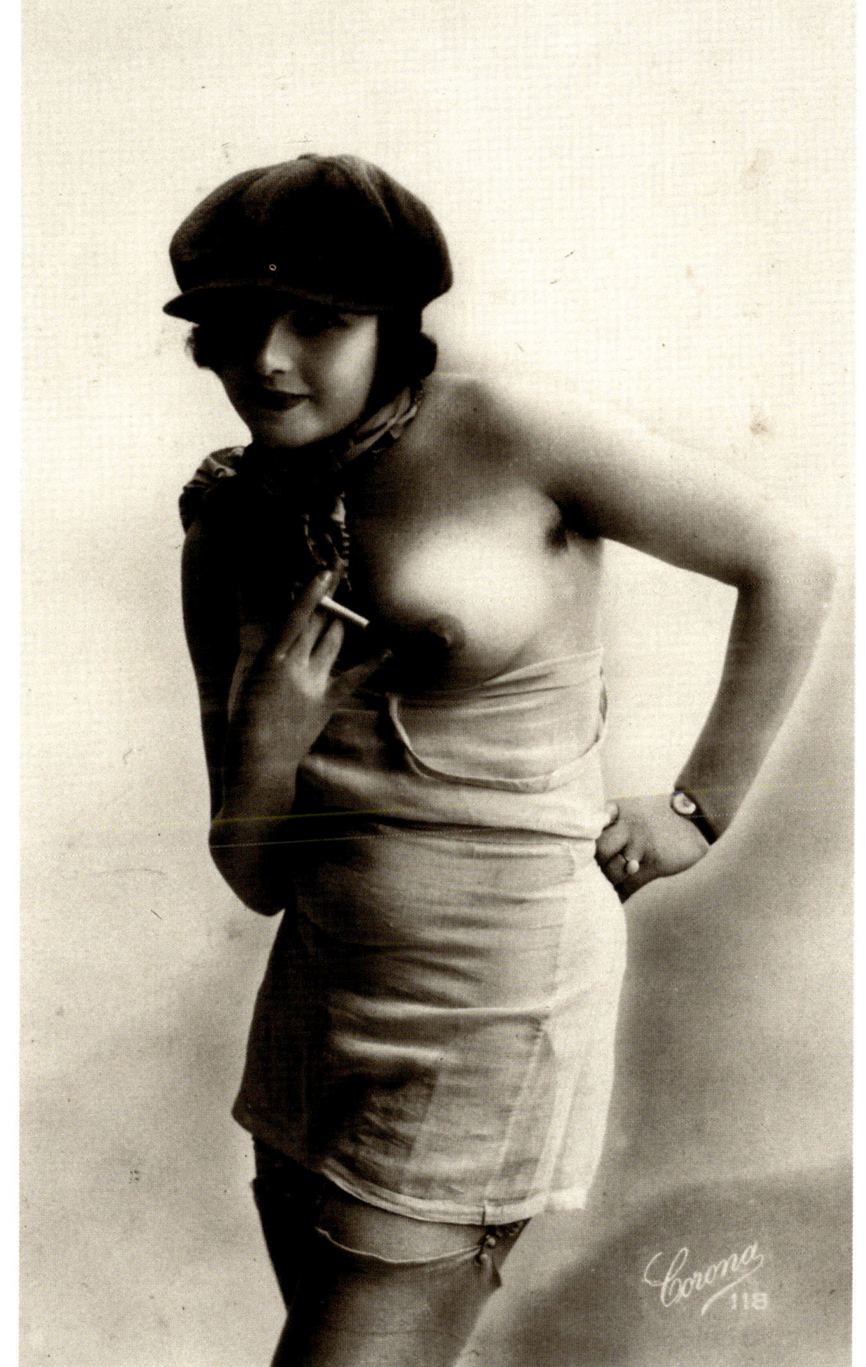
Corona
118

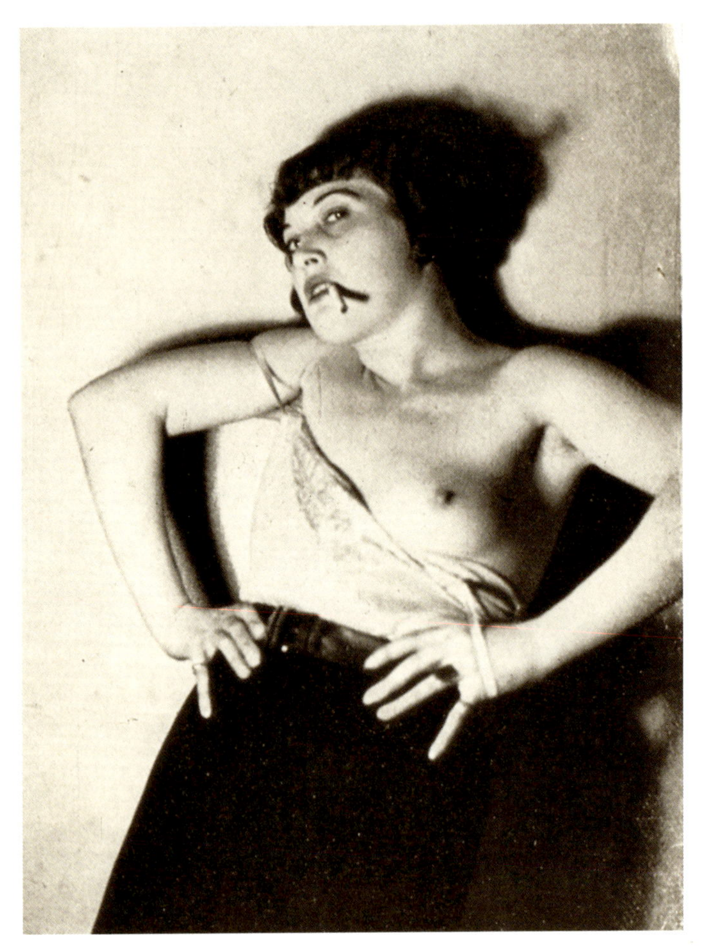

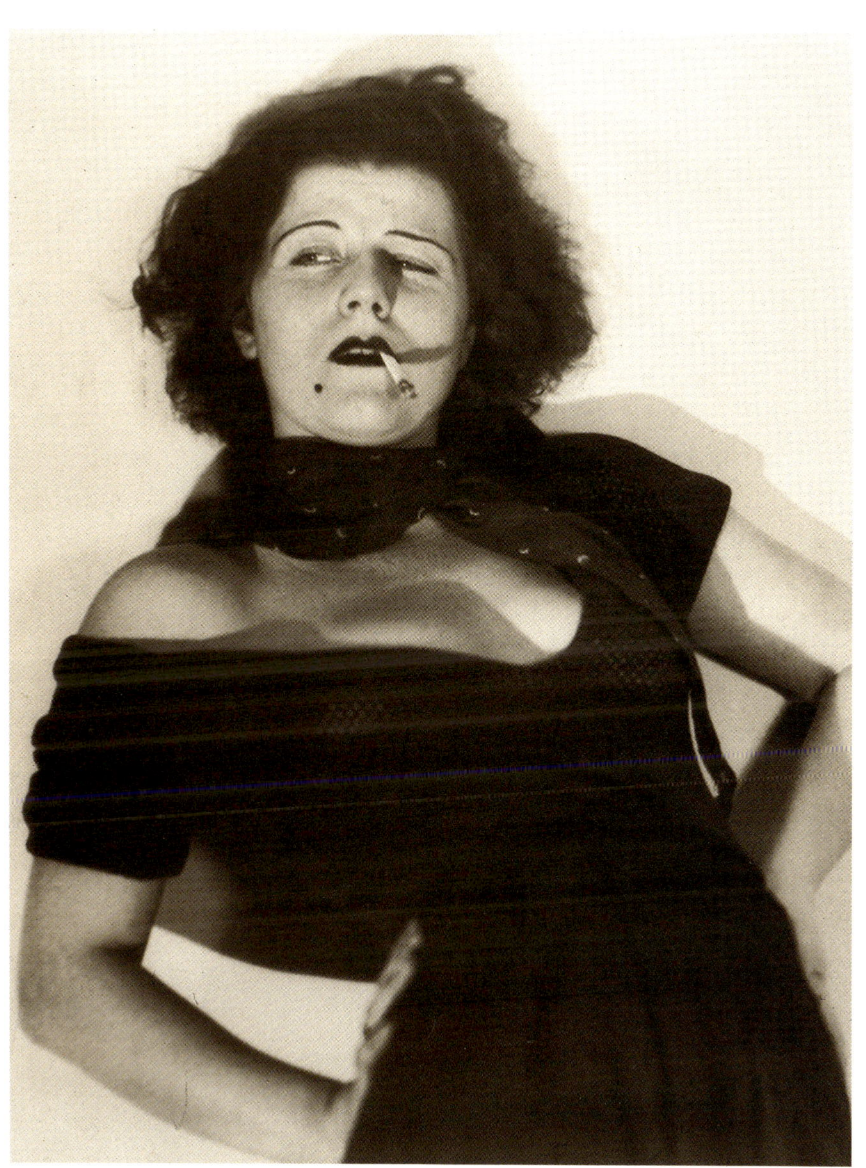

Too much restraint certainly is a mistake.

Alfred de Musset

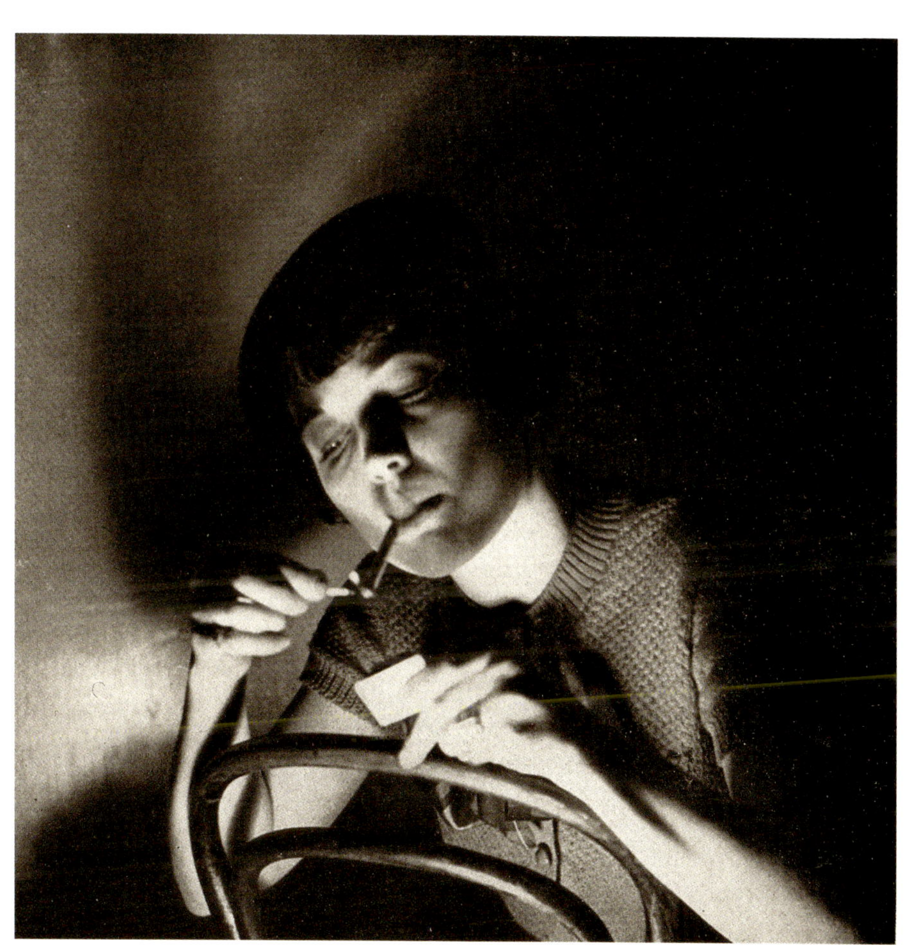

She did not know whether she regretted
having let him love her,
or whether she wanted
to love him even more.

Gustave Flaubert

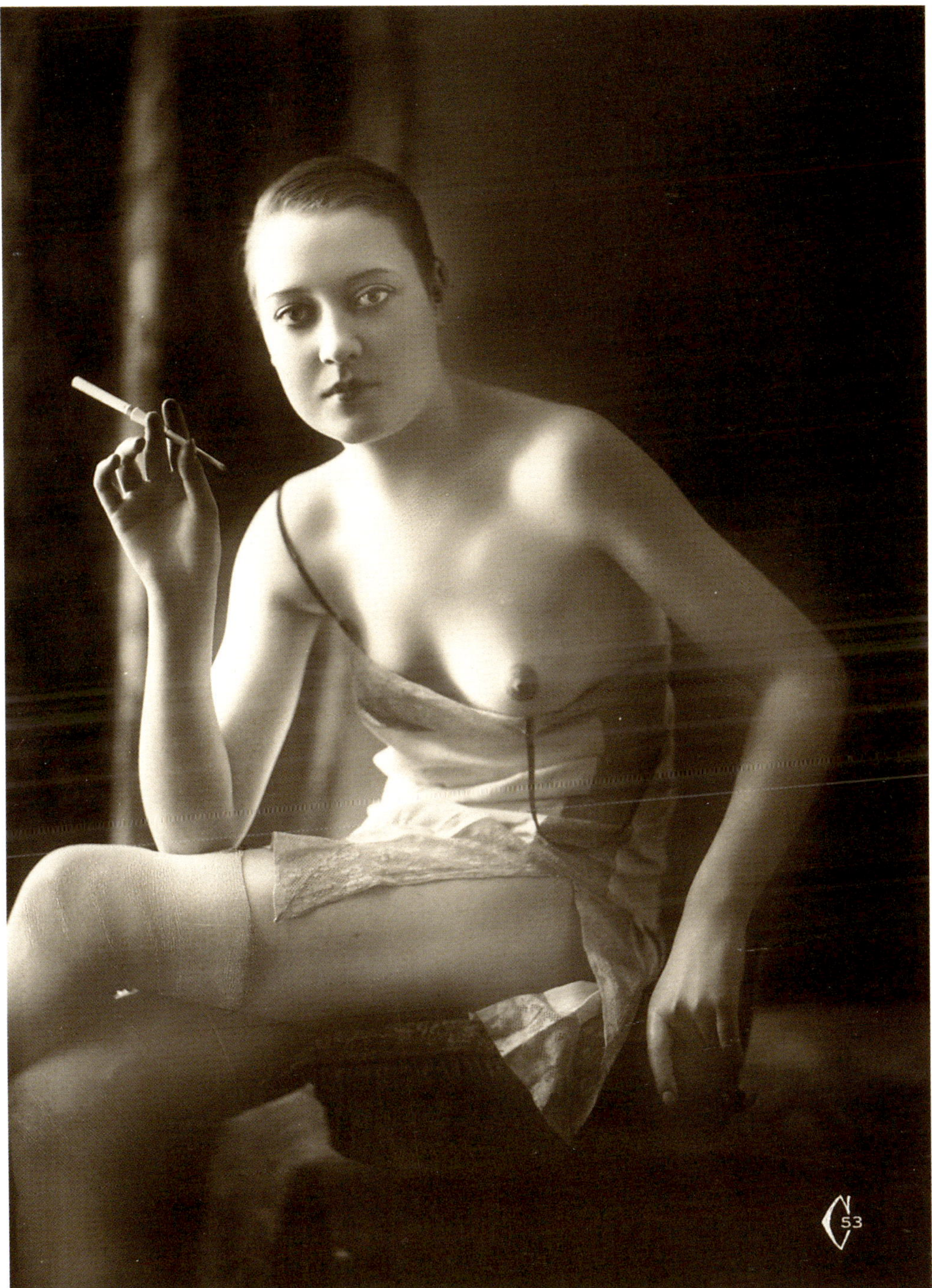
53

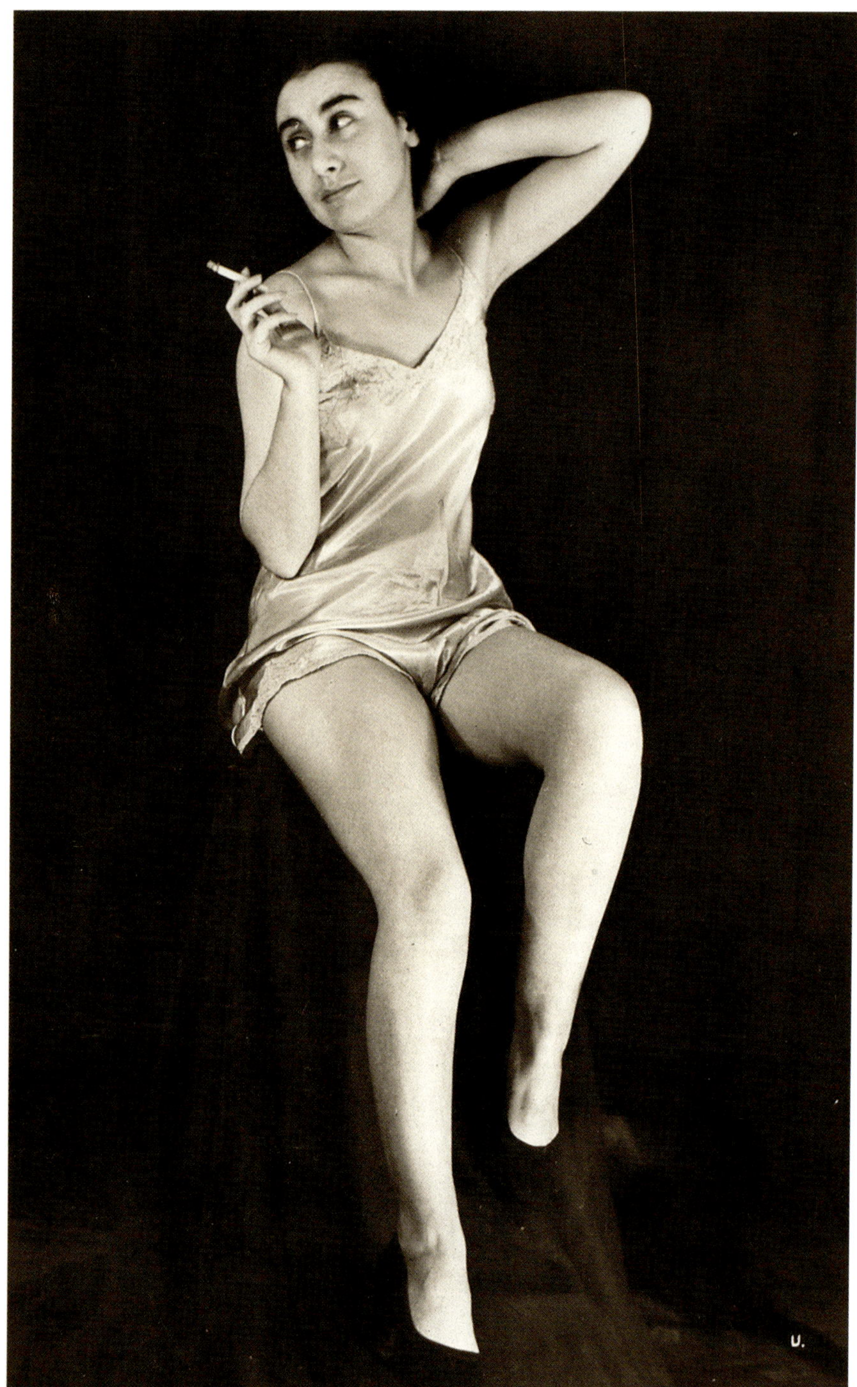
U.

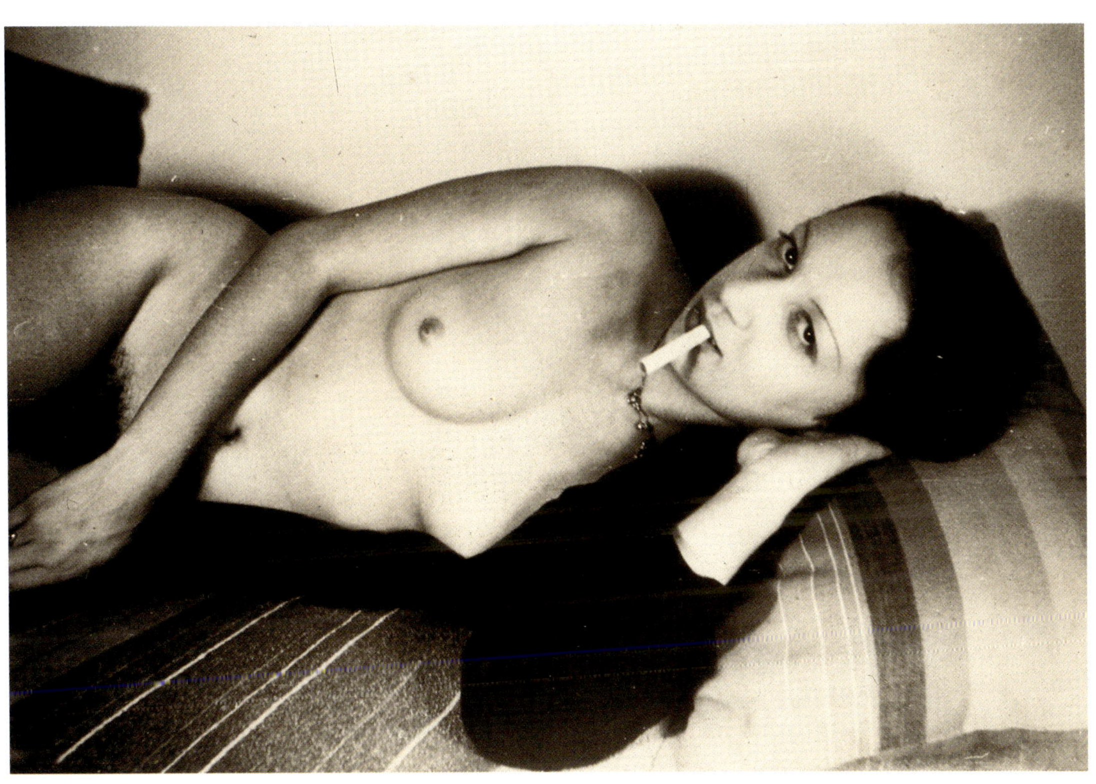

All our moral mistakes merely exist in our minds, with one exception – crime.

Jean-Jacques Rousseau

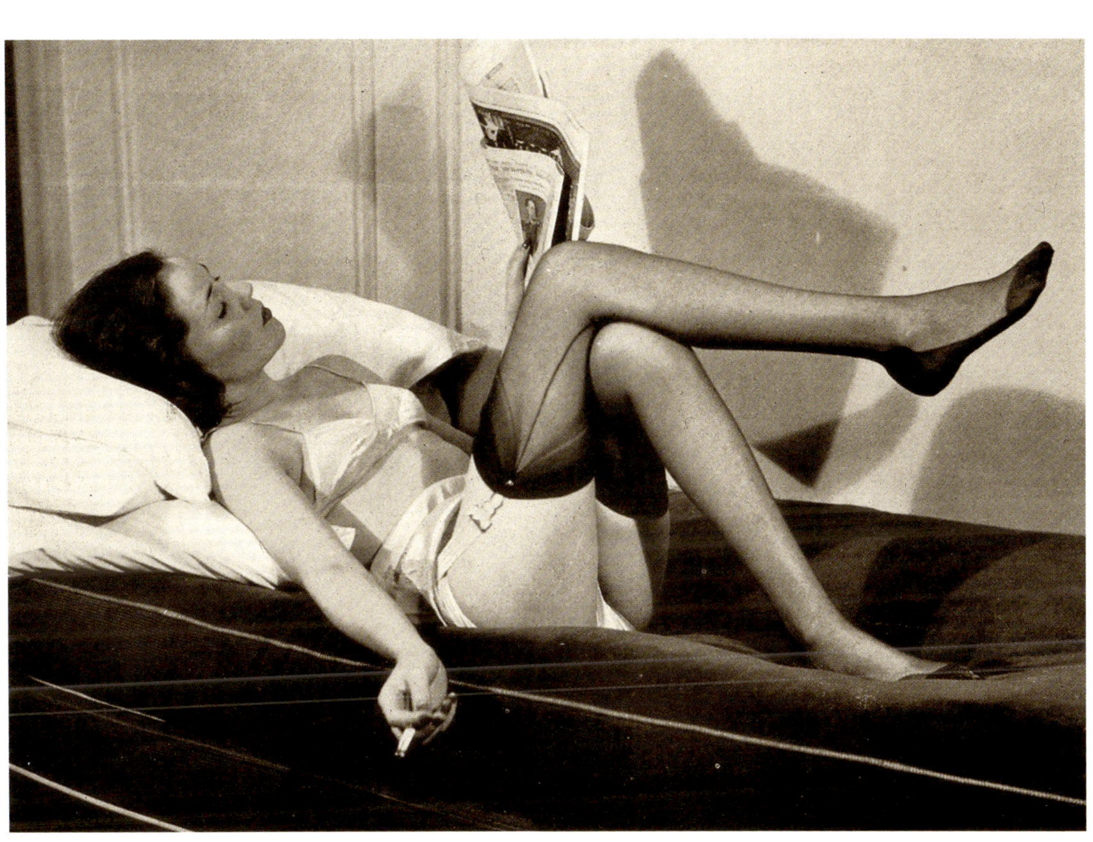

Bibliography

The bibliography confines itself to volumes consulted. Comprehensive surveys of the literature specific to the theme of nude photography/erotica can be found in (among others) Fabian/Freyermuth (1984), Köhler/Barche (1985) and Frank Heidtmann: *Bibliographie der Photographie. Deutschsprachige Publikationen der Jahre 1839 – 1984.* Second revised and expanded edition. Munich/London/New York/Paris, 1989.

Nude Photography and Erotica

Aktphotographie: Die Internationale Bibliothek der Photographie. Zurich, 1984.
Das Bild des Körpers. Schaffhausen, 1993.
Jean-Pierre Bourgeron (Ed.): *Nude 1900.* New York, 1980.
Bilderlust. Erotische Photographien aus der Sammlung Uwe Scheid. Heidelberg, 1991.
Patrice Boussel: *Erotisme et Galanterie au 19e siècle.* Paris, 1979.
Die erotische Daguerreotypie. Sammlung Uwe Scheid. With an introduction by Grant B. Romer. 2nd edition Weingarten, 1990.
Gillo Dorfles: *Der Kitsch.* Gütersloh, 1977.
Die Erotik in der Photographie. Die geschichtliche Entwicklung der Aktphotographie und des erotischen Lichtbildes und seine Beziehung zur Psychpathia sexualis. Vienna/Berlin/Leipzig, 1931.
Monika Faber: *Madame d'Ora Wien – Paris. Portraits aus Kunst und Gesellschaft 1907 – 1957.* Vienna/Munich, 1983.
Monika Faber: *Die montierte Frau. Aktphotographien des Atelier Manassé aus den 20er und 30er Jahren.* Vienna, 1988.
Rainer Fabian/Gundolf S. Freyermuth: *Der erotische Augenblick.* Hamburg, 1984.
Pierre de Fenoyl (Ed.): *Chefs-d'œuvre des photographes anonymes au XXe siècle.* Paris, 1982.
Fotografien auf Postkarten. Aus der Sammlung Robert Lebeck. Essen, 1977.
Glanz und Elend des Körpers/Splendeurs et Misères du Corps. Bern, 1988.
Happy Birthday Photography. Bokelberg Sammlung. Zurich, 1989.
Barbara Jones/William Oulette (Eds.): *Erotische Postkarten.* Cologne, 1977.
Philippe Jullian: *Le nu 1900.* (Ed. André Barret, Paris, 1976)
Michael Köhler: *Akte. Die Geschichte der erotischen Fotografie.* Munich, 1991.
Michael Köhler: *Le nu dans la photographie 1840 – 1986.* Schaffhausen, 1987.
Michael Köhler/Gisela Barche (Eds.): *Das Aktfoto. Ästhetik, Geschichte, Ideologie.* Munich, 1985.
Michael Koetzle/Uwe Scheid: *Naughty Paris. Erotic Photographs of the Twenties.* Cologne, 1994.
Robert Lebeck (Ed.): *Leopold Reutlinger – Die Schönen von Paris. Fotografien aus der Belle Epoque.* Dortmund, 1981.
Robert Lebeck: *Salon de Paris. Erotische Postkarten.* Munich, 1983.
Robert Lebeck/Gerhard Kaufmann: *Viele Grüße... Eine Kulturgeschichte der Postkarte.* Dortmund, 1985.
Jorge Lewinski: *The naked and the nude.* New York, 1987.
Bernard Marbot/André Rouille: *Le corps et son image.* (Ed. Contrejour, Paris, 1986)
Peter Mendes/Graham Ovenden: *Victorian Erotic Photography.* London, 1973.
Serge Nazarieff: *Early Erotic Photography.* Cologne, 1993.
Serge Nazarieff: *Le nu stéréoscopique 1850 – 1930.* Paris, 1985.
Le Nu. Paris, 1986.
Daniela Palazzoli: *Reflections of Life.* (Ed. Idea Books, Milan, 1989).
Daniela Palazzoli: *Il Corpo scoperto. Il Nudo in fotografia.* Milan, 1988.
Regards sur la photographie en France au XIXe Siècle. 180 chefs-d'œuvre de la Bibliothèque nationale. Paris, 1980.
Uwe Scheid: *Das erotische Imago. Der Akt in frühen Photographien.* Dortmund, 1984.
Uwe Scheid: *Das erotische Imago II.* Dortmund, 1986.
Constance Sullivan: *Nude photographs 1850 – 1980.* New York, 1980.
Thomas Walter: *Nudes of the '20s and '30s.* London, 1976.

Smoking and the New Woman

Sigrun Anselm/Barbara Beck (Eds.): *Triumph und Scheitern der Metropole. Zur Rolle der Weiblichkeit in der Geschichte Berlins.* Berlin, 1987.
Ursula A. J. Becker: *Geschichte des modernen Lebensstils. Essen, Wohnen, Freizeit, Reisen.* Munich, 1990.
Georg Böse: *Im Blauen Dunst. Eine Kulturgeschichte des Rauchens.* Stuttgart, 1957.
Huguette Bouchardeau: *Göttern und Teufeln zum Trotz. Das Leben der George Sand.* Munich, 1991.
Grazietta Butazzi: *Die Femme fatale.* In: *Anziehungskräfte. Variété de la Mode 1786 – 1986.* Munich, 1986, pp. 140 – 145.

Egon Cesar Conte Corti: *Die trockene Trunkenheit. Ursprung, Kampf und Triumph des Rauchens.* Leipzig, 1930.
Otto Dix – Menschenbilder. Gemälde, Aquarelle, Gouachen und Zeichnungen. Stuttgart, 1982.
Regine and Peter Engelmeier (Eds.): *Film und Mode. Mode im Film.* Munich, 1990.
Femmes en vue. Photographies Henri Manuel, Felix Nadar, Paul Nadar, Constant Puyo. Paris, 1988.
Christian Ferber (Ed.): *Die Dame. Ein deutsches Journal für den verwöhnten Geschmack 1912 – 1943.* Frankfurt am Main/Berlin/Vienna, 1980.
Frauenalltag und Frauenbewegung im 20. Jahrhundert. 4 Vols. Frankfurt am Main, 1981.
Ute Frevert: *Frauen-Geschichte. Zwischen bürgerlicher Verbesserung und Neuer Weiblichkeit.* Frankfurt am Main, 1986.
Fritz Giese: *Girl-Kultur.* Munich, 1925.
Margarete Gröner: *Bubikopf.* In: *Anziehungskräfte. Variété de la Mode 1786 – 1986.* Munich, 1986, pp. 69 – 71.
F.C. Gundlach/Uli Richter: *Berlin en vogue. Berliner Mode in der Photographie.* Tübingen/Berlin, 1993.
Hart und Zart. Frauenleben 1920 – 1970. Berlin, 1990.
Jost Hermand/Frank Trommler: *Die Kultur der Weimarer Republik.* Munich, 1978.
Elsa Hermann: *So ist die neue Frau.* Hellerau, 1929.
Florence Hervé (Ed.): *Geschichte der deutschen Frauenbewegung.* Cologne, 1987.
Jutta Hülsewig-Johnen: *Neue Sachlichkeit – Magischer Realismus.* Bielefeld, 1990.
Annemarie Hürlimann/Alois Martin Müller (Eds.): *Film Stills. Emotions Made in Hollywood.* Stuttgart, 1992.
Ich und die Stadt – Mensch und Großstadt in der deutschen Kunst des 20 Jahrhunderts. Berlin, 1987.
Rudolf Käs/Helmut Poll: *Die Neue Frau.* In: *Aufriss.* Year I, no. 2, pp. 68 – 69.
Rudolf Käs: *Die Zigarette – der flüchtige Genuß.* In: *Aufriss.* Year I, no. 2, pp. 6 – 24.
Rudolf Kinzel: *Die Modemacher. Die Geschichte der Haute Couture.* Vienna/Darmstadt, 1990.
John Kobal: *Hollywoods Ruhm und Schönheit. The famous "John Kobal Collection". Die hohe Kunst der Glamour-Fotografie.* Munich, 1983.
Ivo Kranzfelder: *George Grosz 1893 – 1959.* Cologne, 1994.
Helene Lange: *Die Frauenbewegung in ihren gegenwärtigen Problemen.* Leipzig, 1924.
Anthony Lipmann: *Der Dandy als Designer. Ernst Dryden – Plakatkünstler und Modeschöpfer.* Munich, 1989.
Jane Livingston: *Lee Miller. Photographer.* London, 1989.
Ingrid Loschek: *Mode im 20. Jahrhundert. Eine Kulturgeschichte unserer Zeit.* Munich, 1984.
Francine Mallet: *Die Muse der Republik. George Sand 1804 – 1876.* Stuttgart, 1979.
André Maurois: *Das Leben der George Sand.* Munich, 1977.
Metropolen machen Mode. Haute Couture der 20er Jahre. Berlin, 1977.
Emanuele L. M. Meyer: *Das Weib als Persönlichkeit.* Zurich/Leipzig, 1924.
Eckhard Neumann (Ed.): *Bauhaus und Bauhäusler. Erinnerungen und Bekenntnisse.* Cologne, 1985.
Anthony Penrose: *The Lives of Lee Miller.* London, 1985.
Kurt Pohlisch: *Tabak. Betrachtungen über Genuß- und Rauschpharmaka.* Stuttgart, 1954.
Gerd Presler: *Glanz und Elend der 20er Jahre. Die Malerei der Neuen Sachlichkeit.* Cologne, 1992.
Reinhold Rauh: *Lola Montez. Die königliche Mätresse.* Munich, 1992.
Ilse Reicke: *Frauenbewegung und -erziehung.* Munich, 1921.
Anna Rheinsberg (Ed.): *Bubikopf. Aufbruch in den Zwanzigern.* Darmstadt, 1988.
August Sander: *Menschen des 20. Jahrhunderts. Portraitphotographien 1892 – 1952.* Munich, 1980.
Wolfgang Schivelbusch: *Das Paradies, der Geschmack und die Vernunft. Eine Geschichte der Genußmittel.* Munich, 1980.
Rudolf Schlichter 1890 – 1955. Berlin, 1984.
Walter Serner: *Gesammelte Werke in zehn Bänden.* Edited by Thomas Milch. Munich, 1988.
Simplicissimus. Eine satirische Zeitschrift. München 1896 – 1944. Munich, 1977.
Kristine von Soden/Maruta Schmidt (Eds.): *Neue Frauen. Die zwanziger Jahre.* Berlin, 1988.
Katharina Sykora/Annette Dorgerloh et al. (Eds.): *Die Neue Frau. Herausforderung für die Bildmedien der Zwanziger Jahre.* Marburg, 1993.
Tendenzen der Zwanziger Jahre. Berlin, 1977.
Margit Twellmann: *Die deutsche Frauenbewegung. Ihre Anfänge und erste Entwicklung 1843 bis 1889.* Meisenheim, 1972.
Frank van Deren Coke: *Avantgarde Fotografie in Deutschland 1919 – 1939.* Munich, 1982.
Palmer White: *Paul Poiret 1879 – 1944. Ein Leben für Mode und Kunst in Paris.* Herford, 1989.
Renate Wiggershaus (Ed.): *George Sand. Geschichte meines Lebens. Auswahl aus ihrem autobiografischen Werk.* Frankfurt am Main, 1978.
Kerstin Wilhelms (Ed.): *Memoiren der Lola Montez.* Frankfurt am Main, 1986.
Elisabeth Wilson: *In Träume gehüllt. Mode und Modernität.* Hamburg, 1989.